p 98

LIVING WITH A
LEARNING DISABILITY

BARBARA CORDONI
Foreword by Sylvia O. Richardson, M.D.

Southern Illinois University Press
Carbondale and Edwardsville

Printed in the United States of America

Edited by Joyce Atwood

Designed by Richard Hendel

Production supervised by Natalia Nadraga

Library of Congress Cataloging-in-Publication Data

Cordoni, Barbara.

  Living with a learning disability.

  Bibliography: p.

  1. Learning disabled youth—Education—United States.

2. Learning disabled youth—United States—Family

relationships.   3. Social skills—United States.

I. Title.

LC470474.C67   1987   649.7'8   87-4473

ISBN 0-8093-1394-4

ISBN 0-8093-1393-6 (pbk.)

The paper used in this publication meets the minimum requirements of American

National Standard for Information Sciences – Permanence of Paper for

Printed Library Materials, ANSI Z39.48-1984. ∞™

This book is dedicated to my children; to Lance and Tara, whose learning problems got me into this field; to Mark and Heather, who supported their brother and sister as we struggled; to my dear husband, Greg, whose caring support enabled this book to be written; to Dr. Sylvia Richardson, my true mentor and friend, whom I will always strive to emulate; to my wonderful mother, who above all others was there when I needed her and whose suggestions were always helpful; to my dear father, whose careful editing and insistence on concise readability helped this book to mature; and finally, to all those students whose lives and development I have been allowed to share.

I once asked Tara if she had ever resented the sometimes limited time I had for her because of the work I was doing for others. Her answer was: "No, Mama. They were all my sisters; they were all my brothers." And indeed, they are.

CONTENTS

FOREWORD

by Sylvia O. Richardson, M.D.

Current literature on learning disabilities is replete with recommendations for alternative methods of teaching academic skills, especially to elementary school children with learning disabilities. This excellent volume is unique. It looks at life after school. It presents the kinds of adaptations needed for educating, communicating with, and parenting the adolescent and young adult with learning disabilities.

In the first naive gush of enthusiasm that greeted the early research into learning disabilities, in the late 1940s and early 1950s, it was easy to accept the glib assurance that learning disabilities could be "cured." It was believed that proper early diagnosis and an appropriate educational or remedial program would "take care of" the learning disabilities by adolescence.

We now know better. In fact, the adolescents and adults with learning disabilities have taught us that academic subjects are not the only hurdle they face. Living skills are as important as skills in the three R's.

Immersed in concern about the specific learning disabilities of their children, parents and teachers tend to forget that these adolescents share the same kinds of problems and need the same strong guidance as any other adolescent. Because of their intense focus on the learning problems per se, too often parents and teachers overlook the significance of social relationships. We fail to recognize that social disability can cause greater pain than difficulty with academic learning.

This book presents a three-dimensional view of the implications of learning disabilities on life after school. The author speaks as a mother, a special educator, and as a friend. Dr. Cordoni has taught all age groups as a learning disability specialist. She established one of the first programs for learning disabled college students at Southern Illinois University. Most of her graduates have gone on to productive lives in many fields, including medicine. She knows whereof she speaks. She writes with clarity, humor, understanding, and deep compassion. The book contains a treasure trove of examples, case histories, and ways to deal with the problems presented. It should be required reading for all families and teachers who live with individuals who have learning disabilities.

LIVING WITH A

LEARNING
DISABILITY

1 LAZY IS A FOUR-LETTER WORD

Virtually every book on learning disabilities begins with a history of the development of the field, but to the parent or the child with L.D., the important topic is not how it began but how it will end. The emphasis of this book is on the adolescent and adult with L.D. and the implications of those learning disabilities on the rest of his life after school. All reported research is listed in the reference section.

A definition of specific learning disabilities, as suggested by the Board of Directors of the Association for Children and Adults with Learning Disabilities (1984), is "a chronic condition of presumed neurological origin which selectively interferes with the development, integration, and/or demonstration of verbal and/or non-verbal abilities. Specific Learning Disabilities exist as a distinct handicapping condition in the presence of average to superior intelligence, adequate sensory and motor systems, and adequate learning opportunities. The condition varies in its manifestations and in degree of severity. Throughout life, the condition can affect self-esteem, education, vocation, socialization, and/or daily living activities."

The male pronoun is used throughout when talking about L.D. people because male sufferers are more prevalent than are females, and to continue to say him/her or he/she is too cumbersome. In contrast, the chapter on parenting refers primarily to the female pronoun because in most instances the L.D. person spends more time with the mother than with the father.

There are many types of learning disabilities. Most often, the difference between what parents and teachers think a child should be achieving and the level at which he is actually achieving is the first clue that something may be wrong. He seems bright and expresses himself well, but in kindergarten he has trouble learning the alphabet or its associated sounds. He may be clumsy and have trouble holding his pencil. He may lean on people because he is unsure of where he is in space. He may ask inappropriate questions because he is impulsive and doesn't realize that there is a time and place for everything.

Later on, he may have trouble learning to read those alphabet symbols as they are formed into words. This condition is called dyslexia, a difficulty with reading and one of the most prevalent of the learning disabilities.

Another person may have no trouble remembering the sounds of the letters but simply cannot control his pencil to the degree necessary to put them down on paper in a form that others can read. Writing is difficult for him, slow, and labored; and his school work is rarely finished on time. He spends most of his recesses finishing the work other children finished long ago. This child has dysgraphia, a difficulty with the visual-motor process called writing.

One individual reads very well, but mathematics is his nemesis. Although he loves his science and reading classes, when it is math time he can't stay in his seat and causes all sorts of trouble in class. He does not understand the symbol system of mathematics and finds a great deal of frustration with this class. He doesn't understand why he is so good in science and has such trouble with math. He is a person with dyscalculia, difficulty with mathematics.

A given individual may have one or several areas that are very hard for him, such as problems in understanding what people are telling him to do. To others, it may seem that he is not paying attention. In these language related disorders, a person may understand some of what is said to him, but not all, causing others to accuse him of not paying attention. Conversely, he may understand what is said but can't remember it long enough to do what he has been told. Another may know and understand what he is to do but cannot tell you about it, for his expressive skills are affected. These and other problems may last into adulthood, affecting him in many ways, denying him access to the world of adult achievement. The difficulties in various academic areas keep him from pursuing vocational goals, without remediation.

→The area of social skills may not develop adequately because of the constant disapproval of others, and because most social skills are learned visually. Since he may not learn well visually, he may seem to be out of touch with reality, or terribly naïve, or not too bright, when really he is simply not comprehending social signals that are quite clear to others.

→ The learning disabled individual is a paradox, doing some things very well and others poorly. He has an average or above-average intelligence. He is not retarded, with a below-average IQ. He has no observable differences from anyone else, and that is why learning disabilities have so often been called the hidden handicap. Yet he is often ridiculed for things he cannot do. For him, as my assistant once said, "Lazy is a four-letter word."

Much of the material presented here was taken from my own experiences as a resource room teacher, as the mother of two children with learning disabilities, Lance and Tara, and from the Achieve Program students.

→The Achieve Program at Southern Illinois University is a support program for students with learning disabilities who want to earn college degrees. I began the Achieve Program at Southern Illinois University in 1978 and was awarded the first federal grant for such a program at a major university in 1980. The success of the program was so significant that the university institutionalized the program in 1983, making it a permanent part of the university structure and distinguishing it as the first L.D. program to be incorporated into a university.

Students are chosen for the Achieve Program on a first come, first served basis. Application forms are filled out, and the student is invited to the university for an interview and two full days of diagnostic testing. These tests help to determine whether we have the program that will enable the student to be successful and what kinds of remedial and supportive services he will need. Criteria include the previous diagnosis of L.D., an average or above-average IQ, and the desire to further his education.

Tutors are tested, interviewed, and trained before they are assigned to students. Graduate assistants are hired and trained to supervise the tutors and the students. The graduate students, who are excellently trained, caring people, form the backbone of the whole Achieve structure. Sally DeDecker, the assistant coordinator, was one of the first. Other fine ones are also mentioned in this book, Heather, Patti, Phyllis, Ellen, Marshall. I have been privileged to work with the best; and although they are not mentioned, they include Anne, Kim, Ernie, Henrietta, Deb, Mary, Terry, Ginny, and Susan. Some have gone on to direct college programs of their own.

Many of the experiences discussed in this book are from the lives of my Achieve students. Their own names are used only when they have desired it. Many of the students have been open, sharing their feelings and emotions with me and with Sally.

The social aspects of a person's life are important at every stage of life, and socialization skills are a major concern for many of my students. These skills affect how easily we handle relationships, jobs, marriages, and parenting—in short, those areas that are most important to all of us. That the social area of learning disabilities is, in many ways, more important than the academic area has only recently been recognized. Rarely is it treated. It needs to be, with as much effort as we apply to academic subjects or even more.

It should be clearly understood that just as all persons with learning disabilities do not have reading problems, not all have socialization problems either. Some L.D. people are completely comfortable in society. This book is not for or about them.

For those experiencing difficulties in social areas, the problem can impact on much of their lives. It is for them and those who love and teach them that this book is written.

2

INAPPROPRIATE!
I'M SO SICK OF
THAT WORD!

Numerous books present detailed analyses of learning disabilities that need not be repeated here. It does seem necessary, however, to discuss briefly the various types of learning disabilities and to characterize a person with L.D. for those readers who may know little about either. Of major concern are those specific disabilities that constitute barriers against the socialization of the individual.

The socialization of an individual begins at birth. Almost daily, little indicators of human behavior begin to emerge. The infant learns to smile; tiny hands and feet wave wildly in the air when someone comes to pick him up. As he grows, he first learns to play by himself, then beside another child, and finally, it is hoped, with another. While all this is happening, he is also learning how to interact with others through his social unit, the family.

For those with learning disabilities, this process can be hindered by the impact of their specific problems. Children with L.D. are often set apart from their peer groups because of their different behavior. Sometimes they are seen as clumsy, and no one likes to be bumped or stepped on all the time. Often, they do not know what to say, or they say what is inappropriate. When a child with L.D. walks up to someone and says, "Why are you so tall?" he is merely asking a question because he is curious, he really wants to know. To the person asked, the question may be offensive. Because of their distractibility and short attention spans, L.D. children tend to disrupt family gatherings and certainly their classrooms. Family members may ridicule their behavior and question the parents' abilities in child rearing. School reports tend to be negative. Add to these problems the academic difficulties and there are few places where either parents or child can feel good about themselves. It is hard for parents and their children to feel wrong or inadequate all the time; but unless something is done, the stage is set for disappointment and frustration.

As children grow, they are expected to learn behavioral and verbal skills. They are expected to know what to say and to whom. Body language, facial expression, and social gestures must be understood in order for an individual to find his place in a social world. Unfortunately, although these are skills we all must learn, they are rarely consciously taught. There are many things which can impact on the L.D. person's ability to acquire social skills. His reaction to those around him, and the reaction of others to him, are the basis for feelings of worth or inadequacies just as they are for all people. Yet, the L.D. person may be limited in his ability to acquire meaning from information that the rest of us take for granted, and as a result, is set apart for reasons he neither understands nor can control.

As parents, teachers, brothers, and sisters, we teach, in very subtle ways, how an L.D. person is to feel about himself. No book can detail every type of disability and how it develops, but it is important to realize that there are specific types of difficulties, each of which contributes to the lack of development of social skills.

THE INFLUENCE OF PARENTS

People with learning disabilities tend to mature emotionally more slowly than their nonhandicapped peers. Partly because of this faltering, many parents fall into the trap of doing more for the child than they should. Although the child may be allowed to do more for himself as he matures, he will still be doing much less than his nonhandicapped peers. The result is an immature adolescent and adult, unable to function adequately in the adult world.

Over and over again, parents have said to me: "What will happen to him when we die? He has no friends. We are his only companions. He has a self-concept you could slide under the door."

My question then must be: "How are you contributing to the problem?"

We called a prospective student's home to find out which one of the testing days he and his parents had chosen in preparation for enrolling in the Achieve Program at Southern Illinois University. I identified myself to the person answering the phone and heard dead silence. That made me certain that the person on the other end was my prospective student.

"Steve, Steve, is that you?"

"My mother said I wasn't to talk to you or take any message," he said.

"Oh," I said, "I will call back later."

I knew what had happened; that mother desperately wanted her son in our program and wanted to take no chance on a garbled message. It happens often, and I understand that, but why wasn't he taught how to take messages years ago, so that he would not be set apart now, in yet another way, from his peers? Steve has learned how to be helpless, and it will impact on much of his life. We criticize our people for their immaturity while we do everything for them. I always know I am in trouble when a student and parent come in for an interview and the conversation goes like this:

Me: "George, have you decided what you want to study?"
Parent: "He doesn't know yet."
*Me: "George, what do you think is your biggest problem in
    school?"*
Parent: "He doesn't do well in English."

Okay, but learned helplessness is hard to unteach.

Keith was very good at writing. He was clever and creative, but he had trouble monitoring his own errors. We were trying to teach him that skill. He was also used to having things done for him, and was not pleased with us for insisting he do his own work. A paper was due, and we were working on it with him. He was to take it home over vacation and develop it, bringing back his work.

He brought it back, all right, finished. His father had written it for him.

As parents and teachers, we must begin to understand what we are doing when we take messages for them, write their papers, and thus demand far less of them than they are capable of being. How are they ever to grow up, to take responsibility for their own actions, unless we slowly, carefully wean them and teach them the skills for adult life? Surely, when we treat them in this way, we are also saying, "I have to do this for you because you are not capable." Perhaps they are not fully capable at this point, but they will never be unless we love them enough to make them try. Pity is a weapon against their growth, but tough love helps them grow.

Tough love. My L.D. daughter, Tara, was poorly organized. She was somewhat socially inept as an adolescent and not doing well in school, either. I tried to organize her, having her put out everything she would need for the next day the night before. It helped some, but did not solve the problem. Almost daily, she would call me to run home and get a book or a paper she had forgotten. One day, I quietly told her that I was sorry about her paper, but that I would not go home to get it. I had already passed English; it was her responsibility to remember her own work. She was furious with me, crying and telling me about her lowered grade and so on. I held firm. I felt like a mean mother, of course; I did not ever want to add to the pain I knew she already had, but neither did I want a thirty-five-year-old child, unable to have a life of her own. It has to start somewhere, but it isn't fun.

THE ATTITUDES OF OTHERS

The new teacher strode intently into the orientation meeting of teachers at the small-town high school. She had earned her master's degree, with honors, in learning disabilities and had taught before. Her knowledge was formidable, but somehow her education had not prepared her for this.

At each teacher's place were a series of handouts, a grade book, and a lesson plan book, the tools of her trade. Yet, there were none for her as the school's resource room teacher, nor for the teacher of the self-contained class. Although there were empty classrooms in the school building, the L.D. teachers had been placed in the art room and in a corner of the gym, respectively. It was a subtle message regarding the status of the L.D. teachers.

The principal, who was responsible for all of this discrimination, began the meeting. He had not wanted special children in his school and his opening comments reflected his attitude. He began: "Well, teachers, this year we're going to have a bunch of dingalings in our school."

Attitudes. How the attitudes of the people around the person with learning disabilities affect his self-image is a major concern here, as well as the opinion the L.D. person forms about himself as a result of those attitudes. How, we must ask ourselves, can a person with L.D. develop a positive self-concept when such attitudes still exist? The special students at that school are no longer physically locked out at the front door, but they are as surely locked out of the mainstream of that school as if they were.

Imagine the attitudes in the halls and in the mainstreamed classes which the L.D. student must face every day, for, sadly, many teachers will follow the administrator's lead. Some teachers don't know any better, but some do know better and seek to please their boss. So each day, L.D. students must pick up their courage as they pick up their books and go out to face a world sadly lacking in understanding. Their courage must be formidable, or else they have decided there is no hope and they go to school because there is no choice. Ironically, these two coping mechanisms, courage and hopelessness, form the behavior patterns often seen in adolescent and adult L.D.'s. These, in turn, are major concerns of this book, for each contributes to the fabric of the person with learning disabilities and his role in society. We are socialized to a great degree by those around us.

Jerry had a sore throat and went to the Health Service alone, not realizing that he would have to fill out a form. In front of a

room full of other students, the nurse said, "Don't you know how to spell the name of your own dorm?" He left and came to me, his throat untreated and his eyes full of rage. It doesn't seem to stop.
By the time our L.D. students are adolescents, they too often believe that if there is something they can do, it isn't worth doing. Belittling their successes while pointing out their failures, they have assumed the role that others have taught them to assume. There was a beautiful young woman in our program some years ago, who wrote so movingly of her family experiences that I was sometimes overwhelmed. She would not accept praise from us even though it was genuinely given. Not until she had heard it from many people would she at last allow herself to believe that she had some talent. She is writing a book now; I eagerly await it.

It is not at all difficult to understand how these kinds of feelings develop. It starts early with pain. One of our students can learn anything, I think, if he is simply allowed to write notes in his own way, from which to study. He has used this technique for years, and he knows how he learns best. His latest notes for a physics class look like this:

$$
\begin{array}{cccc}
\text{(force)} & = & \text{(mass)} & \times & \text{(acceleration)} \\
* & & \square & & \rightarrow \\
\text{(gravity)} & = & \text{(mass)} & - & \text{(acceleration)} \\
\downarrow & & \square & & \rightarrow
\end{array}
$$

Clever! This dyslexic student can't spell the words but it is certain he understands the concept. As he said, "When I tried to use this technique in school so I would remember, the nuns held my pictures up for all the class to see and laugh at and then tore them up. Those were my notes, so I failed."

Although differences in human response patterns are noted in newborns, the attitudes of those around us are what really teach us in subtle ways just how we are to respond to others, and how we are to feel about ourselves. It is an awesome responsibility to those of us who raise these sons and daughters, love them, teach them, hire them, and live with them.

Just as the message to the L.D. teacher was subtle, so are the messages to those we seek to help; yet those messages can be not only lifelong, but life threatening. We must do it better.

VISUAL PERCEPTION DIFFICULTIES

The majority of things we learn, particularly when we are young, are learned visually. Making a snowball, turning on a faucet, opening a car door, making a toy work, are things we watch others do, then we try ourselves. We are learning by imitation. We learn what social gestures mean—waving goodbye, a crooked finger to "come here," a finger to the lips to "hush." It took me a long time to discover that I had to teach those skills to my L.D. children. My other children had learned them easily while my L.D. children blithely went on with whatever it was they were doing, despite all the messages I thought I was sending them. If these kinds of gestures do not have meaning or are visually confusing, one can hardly be expected to respond to them, but I didn't know that then. I thought I was being ignored, and I didn't like it. We have to learn what a frown means, that raised eyebrows mean someone is asking a question; even a laugh or quizzical look must be defined and understood. The integration of a facial expression with a specific meaning is a difficult task for some people.

BODY LANGUAGE PROBLEMS

Physically, our body language is revealing; we expect certain postures or expressions of those around us. We are expected to know how to sit decorously, to maintain eye contact with someone in a conversation, to walk without bumping into others, and the older we are, the more such knowledge is expected of us. However, because of the nature of the disabilities, many L.D. people do not learn these skills easily. Often, L.D. adults have said to me that they didn't know that a particular posture or facial expression had meaning. It comes as a shock to them that they had missed that clue for so long. Imagine what it must be like to be constantly rejected and never know why!

It is consistently reported that the nonverbal communication in every conversation is far more important than the words themselves. These nonverbal communications are very subtle, and without a visual sensitivity to them, we may appear less than we are. Yet, people with L.D. find these kinds of messages particularly confusing.

Consider how we behave when we wish to end a conversation. Some closing remark is made, such as "Well, I'm glad we had this talk," and then we move; we stand up or at least turn our bodies. Not understanding the implications of these messages, the L.D. person is likely to keep talking or stay seated. In a testing situation, a graduate student completed the last test, put away her stopwatch, gathered her test materials, and stood up. The client stayed in his chair and looked at her expectantly. She finally said, "We're finished, Mitchell." "Oh," he said and stood up. Imagine his problems in a job interview.

TACTILELY DEFENSIVE PROBLEMS

Repeatedly, it has been said that one can spot the L.D. child in kindergarten because he's the one who flunks out at standing in line, and there is a strong element of truth in that statement. People with L.D. often have great difficulty in determining the life space of others. Most people are bothered by someone standing too close to them, yet my L.D. college students will back me and their other professors into a wall. I felt a great sense of relief when my children grew up and learned about such things, when I finally was bright enough to teach them, and they stopped standing on my feet when they wanted to talk to me. For a while there, I swore I was going to buy steel-toed sneakers.

Although my children and I can laugh at such things now, there was a time when it set them apart from their peers and they were very lonely. People shy away from those who are different. A little girl I taught was asked to leave the kindergarten car pool because she had spatial problems and was very unsure of where she was in space. In order to combat this, she touched whomever she was next to at all times. She didn't hit or scratch, she just leaned on them. The mothers of the non-L.D. children and the kindergarten teacher thought this was weird and didn't want to be around her.

A dear friend with L.D. said to me, "Do you mind if I hug you? I'm a very tactile person. I need to touch and reach out to others, but I have learned to ask first because some people don't like it." How do we know if it's the appropriate time and place to hug someone? We make these judgments because we pick up clues from the other person's behavior. If one does not read these clues or attach meaning to them, it becomes an impossible task and one has to learn to ask. I hugged her, of course.

Even the tightness of the hug must be learned. A friend of the opposite sex may be hugged lightly and patted a bit, while a same-sexed friend may be hugged a bit tighter. One of my students hugs everyone, or at least tries to. Her hugs consist of flinging her arms around the person's neck and squeezing so hard she nearly chokes him. She tends to follow the object of her affection around, waiting for an unguarded moment when she can slip in another hug. Her need to touch and hold is very great; it is also inappropriate and very painful. In trying to teach her when and whom to hug, I used the term *inappropriate* too often, I suspect, for she burst out one day with, "Inappropriate, inappropriate, I'm so sick of that word!" She is naturally a very loving, caring person, but until she learns how, when, and to what degree to express those qualities, others are bound to see the outward expression only and not the love behind it. I walked into the learning lab one day to ask her whereabouts. Another student replied, "I don't know. It's not my turn to watch her." So the quality of her life is less than it could be and she does not have that sense of belonging that all people crave. How this affects the emerging adult will be discussed in depth in a later chapter.

RIGIDITY OF THOUGHT

Most of us, most of the time, have the ability to consider another's point of view and to adjust our thinking if we feel that point of view has merit. Among many people who have learning disabilities, such an adjustment is a difficult task. Too often, perhaps, they have their own ideas rejected or downplayed; or confused by what they think they have heard or seen, they may form an opinion that is difficult to change. Add to that problem the normal pattern of most young people to reject adult opinions and there may develop a mind-set of awesome proportions. It can be very difficult to lead them.

Love relationships, when they develop at all, often become so intense that concentrating on anything else is next to impossible. The rigidity of thought causes a problem in seeing another as he really is, and the love object is seen as all good, all caring, all perfect. On the other hand, when one breaks up, the former love becomes all bad. Such situations can be difficult for families.

Opinions pertaining to political elections, the Communists, or any other issue that involves some emotion, are often perceived in the same way. The sadness of this situation for persons with L.D. is that it prohibits discussion of issues with anyone who may think differently.

ADVERSIVENESS

Adversiveness is a condition which causes the person to complain when there is nothing to complain about; to be cross without reason; to take the opposite point of view just because it is the opposite point.

Adversive behavior is unpleasant and can take many forms. Sara said, loudly of course, "I don't like towel-heads in my school!" She was referring to some Indian students who wore turbans. Mark detested his middle eastern professor whom he called a camel jockey. Even though we understand that such adversive comments are caused by the person's own feelings of rejection, or even by the parental values to which he has been exposed, we must still firmly address such behavior.

L.D. students often complain about assignments that are perfectly fair, loudly proclaiming that the professor is out to get them, ignoring the facts that we will help them and that everyone else in class has to do the assignment, too. If it were just the work, one could understand the feelings better, but it may be the time the class is scheduled or the sex of the teacher. Tom was scheduled for tutoring in the evenings because of his class load, the availability of tutors in his subject matter, and so forth. "No way," said he. "I can only meet with a tutor on Tuesday and Thursday in this building between two and four p.m. In the evening there's too much to do."

It is simply not pleasant to be around someone who is cross all the time. Eventually, the normal person seeks to avoid contact with the cross person, but with the learning disabled we must not avoid him. Rather, a frontal attack on his behavior is necessary. If videotaping is available, analyzing the behavior together is an excellent technique for showing him how he appears to others. If video is not available, then behavior must be talked through and an alerting device must be agreed upon. For instance, when my children were little, I used a hand signal which meant, à la Thumper rabbit, "If you can't say something nice, don't say nothin' at all." An L.D. adult I am trying to help now responds to another private signal when he goes on and on about a topic or appears particularly cross.

Rap sessions are uniquely efficient for dealing with adversive behavior. Keeping the group to fifteen participants or so, and including some tutors and graduate students, allows for modeling to take place, where people with L.D. can see how others respond. There are some excellent social skills training programs listed in the reference section, but most are group activities.

There are also a few successful high school programs for students with learning disabilities. These classes form a vehicle where students can sort out feelings and beliefs with supportive help and learn about their disabilities. Some educational therapists have formed groups of their clients to talk through issues such as name calling or responses to minorities. With the young adult, we have found that a major area of concern is male-female relationships. Calling females "broads" is as adversive to most women as "towel-head" or "camel jockey" may be to the foreign-born.

Much of the prejudice in this world has occurred because someone needed to find a scapegoat to blame when something went wrong, or because he needed to feel superior to others in some way. Those who feel inferior in any of many ways often assume a posture that allows them to look down on someone else, whether or not their reason is valid. If people with few problems resort to this behavior regularly, it is not surprising why so many with L.D. do. Only when they begin to appreciate their own real value, does such behavior diminish.

WORTHLESSNESS

Sadly, some people with L.D. grow up feeling that they are somehow incomplete and worthless. Some act out as a result, becoming juvenile delinquents. Others become severely depressed and attempt suicide. Some succeed.

It frightened me when Erin's mother closed the door and quietly told me of his suicide attempts. He was such a great kid, bright and extremely handsome. He was a good athlete, so there was something to feel good about. Still, he had felt too many times that life was not worth living. Through careful training and a great deal of love from an Achieve graduate student, my daughter Heather, he began to like life again, eventually to embrace it joyfully, so it was especially hard for us to lose him in a tragic accident later, but as his mother said to Heather, if it had to happen, thank God it happened when he was happy and feeling good about himself, and that was because of Heather.

Feeling good about themselves is something we must give them, for they are worthy of that, and are as needful as anyone else for that feeling.

Polite society requires specific behavior of us, but if one's eyes wander, if it is difficult to sort out one facial expression from another, if one needs to touch in order to know where one is, then one may appear different or socially inept.

I often do a mental double take at some of the things I hear and see. Don said the other day, "Well, I fell off the deep edge again!" Or the one who fell through the manhole but told me he wasn't hurt "because I am so well coordinated." But my absolute all-time favorite was when I asked a young man what kind of disability he had. His reply was, "I don't remember. I think it was memory."

Throughout this book, I hope you'll be able to see that the use of humor for the person with L.D. and for those around him can be the glue which holds it all together. As Dan said, "You know, I don't really mind having a learning disability. It's just that it takes up so much of my time!" And that's what this book is all about. L.D. needs to be put into perspective. It can impact on every aspect of adolescent and adult life if we let it. It can utterly destroy a life or it can, through proper treatment, become only a minimal irritant. It is manageable; it is only a small part of the person unless we allow it to assume a proportion it does not deserve. It is hoped that this book will help to keep that from happening.

3 IT WOULD TAKE ME TOO HARD
LANGUAGE BASED DISABILITIES

Because of the difficulty in looking at the whole person, it is often easier to look at pieces of the person's behavior. This partial view allows us to look at some possible explanations for some of the isolation that many L.D. people feel.

One of the most pervasive of the learning disabilities is language disorders. Difficulties in understanding what others are saying does not lend itself to good conversation, our major form of personal interaction. Difficulty in expressing oneself may also be a problem, for one has only to walk in any corridor at any high school, the university, or in an office building to find little enclaves of people talking comfortably. The child or adult with an auditory perception problem who cannot understand facial expressions any better than he comprehends the auditory stimuli has no mechanism for understanding how others feel about him. I vividly remember my son Lance's trips to the kitchen once to ask, "Mama, are you mad at me?" Smiling and assuring him I was not, I was surprised to find him back again shortly with the same question. Eventually, I began to wonder if he had done something I didn't know about. By the time he asked the fifth time, I was angry.

This is called a receptive disability. Many with receptive disabilities become accomplished lip readers, depending on visual clues to ensure understanding. This does not mean that there is anything wrong with their ears, it simply means that they do not consistently comprehend what is being said. Adding another sensory system, such as vision, aids comprehension for people with this type of disability. My son was reading my lips for years before I knew what his difficulties were. I learned to take his face in my hands and look at him intently before I told him something.

Even today, he will occasionally experience difficulty if there is a great deal of background noise, such as at a game or in a crowded room.

This misperception of what is said takes different forms. In the young child, we often find difficulties in the pronunciation of words. As adolescents or young adults, pronunciation is rarely a factor, but other language based problems are apparent. I was testing a young man and asked the question, "What would be the thing to do if, while in a movie, you were the first person to see smoke and fire?" He answered, "Well, if I liked the movie, I'd tell my friends."

L.D. people may have other types of language based disabilities as well. Just as my son could not gain meaning from my tone of voice or from the words I used, so others may experience difficulties in these or related areas. Some people with learning disabilities speak too loudly for the situation; others mumble or speak too softly, unable to modulate their voice levels or judge their own pitches. Some tend to speak in a monotone which makes listening to them tedious and their conversations quickly lose our attention. Often, their vocabularies are not extensive, so answers to questions are short and verbally unexciting. On the other hand, they may talk too much, going over and over the same information in a kind of verbal perseveration until no one can bear it anymore. My assistant, Sally, and I were discussing this one day and I said, "You know, Bill has so much to say and can't talk and Joe has so little to say and talks all the time." She replied, "Yes, we are in a working tower of Babel." And so it is. However, Bill had a math teacher who was foreign born. We were concerned about Bill's ability to understand him and said, "Bill, can you understand his lectures?" Bill said, "Well, let's put it this way; I think I can understand him better than he can understand me!" That kid will make it.

I'm not so sure about Virginia. Her father asked to meet me one evening to discuss her many problems. We talked for several hours. Knowing I was to meet him, she later asked what we had talked about. I told her we had talked about her concerns about her major and so forth, to which she responded, "Is that all? You spent all night with him!" Jumping to conclusions can cause trouble. I promise I won't believe everything I hear about you, if you promise you won't believe everything you hear about me!

Comprehension of what is said on a consistent basis is a significant problem for some people. Some report that since they are never quite certain if what they thought they heard was what was really said, they simply respond to everything by smiling and nodding. That could get someone in serious trouble! Others, who have not developed that coping mechanism, have a perpetual quizzical look on their faces. They tend to cock their heads from side to side, frowning and looking puzzled.

It is important to watch your children or students carefully because they will often tell you with their behavior what they may not know themselves. When I am talking or working with a student, I purposely turn away or cover my lips and continue talking. Some will not physically respond, but obviously don't understand what was said. Others will physically rearrange their bodies in an attempt to see my face. If one watches for such things, the knowledge gained can be most helpful in working with them. Helpful, but not foolproof; for I am certain that I never agreed to a slumber party for fourteen hyperactive boys—they came anyway.

Ray wore a perpetually puzzled look on his face. He would cock his head to one side, furrow his brow, and stare at the speaker's face. Now, the normal reaction to this is for the speaker to explain the topic over again using different words, perhaps, but that only confused Ray further. He would frown and continue staring and the speaker would try again. It was very frustrating to all involved, particularly because after he had been told something several times, Ray would attempt to reiterate what had been said. Rarely did it match with what he had been told, but several more times that day he would appear back in the office to say it one more time. We had to spend more time with Ray than with any ten of our other students. Lecture classes, some of which he had to take, were disastrous.

To help him, and ourselves, we started him on note-taking skills. We practiced speaking to him in short sentences, giving only basic facts, and waiting for him to write down key words. When we had completed the discussion on one point, Ray read back to us from his notes so we could check for accuracy. As he became more sure of himself, the puzzled looks appeared less frequently, and to this day he is a prodigious note writer.

Ray had recorded all of his class lectures, bringing them to the lab where he and his tutor would listen to the lecture, taking notes and stopping the tape at key points. Obviously, the amount of time Ray had to spend for each lecture class was triple that of the other class members, but there was no other way. Eventually, he would turn on the recorder in class but would also attempt to take class notes himself. Later in the lab, he and his tutor took notes as they listened to the recorded lecture and then compared Ray's notes from class with them. In this way, Ray also learned to judge what was important to write down and what could be deleted.

After two years, Ray was ready to complete college without Achieve services. He had learned some skills and had developed some coping techniques for other areas of weakness. He is much more self-assured now, but his is a common problem area.

Some people with learning disabilities understand what is said to them but have problems in knowing what to say or when to say it. Clint's tutor was trying to get him to respond to, and to initiate, greetings. One of his first assignments was to go into one of the graduate students' offices to say "hello." Clint walked in and sat down. Marshall looked at him expectantly and Clint said, "Hello," and left. On to lesson two.

Other problems are less severe than Clint's, but just as troublesome in a social world. Another of Marshall's students has learned to nod at the speaker and seems to be understanding the dialogue. He doesn't, of course, and responds with what Marsh calls "generic" responses such as "sure, okay," or "uhuh" and that, too, is a way of coping. One of our girls could be termed the typical valley girl and the quality of her responses is no better than the male student's, but much more obnoxious. "Oh you ___!" is her favorite term. Needless to say, these are not endearing qualities, even though the person cannot correct them at this time without help. Such disabilities severely limit a person's interactions with others, and people just don't want to be around them.

At another level we find the problem of verbal perseveration, wherein the person says the same thing in slightly different words, over and over again. Lloyd used to tell me about a television show, taking as long to tell me the plot as the whole show had run. It was difficult to escape from him.

Those who go on and on about a topic, verbally perseverating and digressing over and over with unnecessary details, can be equally frustrating. One adult L.D. person I know will begin to tell me about a trip to a museum, which I would like to hear about. What I don't want to know is where he parked, what he had for lunch, how it was prepared, sliced, and served! One wants to say, "Who cares? Get on with the museum."

Others, convinced that you will accept their point of view providing you hear it often enough, will follow you around, no matter how many oral and physical cues you give them suggesting that the topic be closed. This can be most frustrating when there is work to be done. Art wanted to drop a class, but since he was quite capable of doing the work, I would not let him. He followed me around all day with the same arguments. Finally he said, "Well, my father says I can drop it," his final weapon against my refusal. It had been a long day, and I blurted out, "Then your father must have less faith in your abilities than I do!" Surprised by my statement, Art kept talking and soon it wasn't Art who wanted to drop the class, it was his father's idea. He stayed in the class and I never did find out whose idea it had really been, but I wished I had said that in the morning!

What is your response when someone talks at great length about a topic you were once interested in but certainly are not any more? Generally, we begin to look around us and shuffle our feet, rather clear messages to those without learning disabilities. L.D. people who have begun to understand such signals will often speak quite rapidly with little continuity in order to get it all said before you get away; this has happened to them before. But, the majority will not perceive these subtle signals. A child who finds himself in such a situation would be likely to say, "Oh, shut up," and walk away disgustedly. Nonhandicapped adults are socialized, with some notable exceptions, and respond much more subtly, which is exactly the technique we must not use with the L.D. person. He needs concrete instructions. In suffering from terminal politeness, we fail to teach as we should.

Sometimes word order, or syntax, is a problem. This difficulty will show up as words in the wrong order within a sentence, such as, "You can both wear them." Faith regularly says "the all" for "all the," and "from far" for "far from." Carol said, "You pick the words I don't know what are." Others simply choose the wrong word or the one of the opposite meaning. "This lemonade is too sweet, pass the sugar." Ed said, "My needs are longer," while Flo stated, "Give me an inch and I'll take a fact!" Jason said he couldn't practice taking notes because "It would take me too hard." Some will take two common phrases and join them together in a most uncommon manner. "The cart before is locking the barn door," a mother said to me. Too often, I'm the one with the quizzical look!

Fortunately, some language therapists are trained to remediate these kinds of difficulties. It is wise to begin such therapy as soon as the problem is noted, in order that there be as little social isolation as possible due to language problems. However, it is never too late to begin. In the Achieve program, students with language deficits are routinely scheduled into therapy. It amazes me how quickly they learn language skills in the hands of a good therapist.

Language usage impacts on every aspect of our lives, but our society allows for some differences between people. Men are sometimes classified as the strong, silent type; a person who is loquacious may be considered enthusiastic or vivacious, or cute, providing they have something to say. We are less likely to accept the weak, silent type or those whom we perceive to be that way. If the silent type answers yes or no, and does not follow through with the conversation, eventually we give up and go on to another person, leaving the silent one as silent and lonely as he was before.

Neither are we patient with those who make unthinking, inappropriate comments. The L.D. person often asks inappropriate questions, inquisitive in nature, such as, "How old are you?" or "How much money do you make?" These are questions the non-handicapped know they should not ask. Some comments relate to another taboo topic, how a person looks. "You need to let me fix your makeup," Randy said to me. "Why? What is wrong with it?" I questioned, a bit unnerved by his statement. "I always used to help my sisters with their makeup. I'll help you," he said, advancing toward me. "No, thank you, Randy," I said, for I had seen his sisters. "I don't wear much makeup and I like it just the way it is." "All right, but you would be prettier if you would just let me help you." Made my day.

Consider the last time you were at a party where someone made an inappropriate remark. What was your reaction? Usually, we turn away to start a conversation with someone else, turning our bodies away as we do so. These are subtle signals and often pass unrecognized by the person with learning disabilities. He does not understand that turning away was a rebuff because we did not approve of what was said. We have to learn to tell him that we did not approve, not a pleasant task since we have been taught to be polite. We have to provide feedback, saying "What you said hurt my feelings. What you could have said was . . . ," or, "It is not polite to ask such a question. If you wanted to know, this is how you could have handled it instead."

Mike had absolutely no trouble talking. The trouble was with what he said, and to whom. Mike was one of our older students, and he had gone with us to a convention in Chicago. The graduate students were planning a wine and cheese party to welcome back graduate students from former years. Mike went to the liquor store with Phyllis to help her carry the wine. No sooner had they begun to look for what they wanted than Mike marched up to the store owner, a tough little man who had run a liquor store in downtown Chicago for half a century. "When are you going to get your store organized?" he asked. The owner may have been prepared for physical assaults but he was not prepared for Mike. "Well?" Mike continued, "It should be patently obvious to anyone with a brain in his head that if the liquor were arranged in alphabetical order, I wouldn't have to walk all over the store to find the wine." Still somewhat subdued by this unexpected attack, the owner mumbled something about seeing his point. Not to be deterred by Phyllis dragging on his arm, Mike continued as she pulled him out the door. "If you see my point, when do you intend to change it?" Mike got feedback all the way to the hotel. Whether you are parent, teacher, other professional, or friend, you need to provide feedback, too. While you may be uncomfortable at first, you will be providing the L.D. person with the only chance he has probably ever had to receive the feedback he needs in order to modify his behavior. The older he gets, the more he will need these skills and the less likely he is to receive the help he needs. He must depend on family members and L.D. specialists to provide it. Don't fail him because of your discomfort.

Some people with learning disabilities have difficulty finding the word they want to use. While each of us experiences this once in a while, it is the constancy of the problem which may set them apart. Many have developed coping mechanisms to help them remember a word, but these mechanisms are often behaviors which are not acceptable in a social world. I have one student who strikes his thigh, hard, with his fist over and over trying to recall; another hits his head with his palm repeatedly. Those guys are viewed as strange in a classroom or in a dorm, for one can hit one's own thigh once or hit one's head once with an exclamation of, "Why can't I think of that word?" and it is acceptable, but to strike oneself over and over is not. Teach such students to substitute another behavior, such as snapping their fingers or a phrase to use such as "I'll think of it as soon as you are gone." If we help them earn their degrees but don't address such behavior, what are their chances of being employed in their fields?

Modulating one's voice is difficult. Some of us naturally talk louder than others. Personality differences, such as shyness, also impact on how softly or loudly we speak, but this is very different from the problems a person with L.D. must face. Those of us without these difficulties tend to modulate our voices depending on the situation and the intimacy of the conversation. To the person with language disorders, neither of these factors may be considered when he wishes to say something. Often, an L.D. person is unaware that sometimes his voice is too loud or too soft. He may speak of the most private family matters in a loud voice at the supermarket. It can be very embarrassing to the family and while we are trying to quiet him, he will be standing there trying to figure out what he did wrong this time.

Sometimes, there appears to be little understanding of polite forms. Ralph was getting better control over his learning disabilities. Sally said, "Have you noticed? Ralph demands differently now. Now he knows what he is demanding instead of just general demanding." I remember the demanding of my children. "Button my dress!" I would hear, to which I learned to respond, "Of course I will help you, but I would feel better if you said please."

Language based disabilities are without question some of the most inhibiting of the learning disabilities because of their impact on so many areas of life. They can, and should, be remediated in each individual regardless of age.

Those children whose verbal-social judgment is also poor may say hurtful or unfeeling things that wound others or make them think the person is a bit strange. Sometimes, what they say is not so bad, it is just impolite. Bob had just moved into the dorm and had only recently met his new roommate. Bob constantly asked him questions. "Do you always sing in the shower? Do you intend to stay up every night? Why do you only wear faded jeans?" Bob's interest and attempts to get acquainted with his roommate were perceived as rudeness and the two did not get along. Sometimes I am just amused. While testing a young man, I asked his birthdate and when he replied that it was December 21, I said, "Oh.

That's my birthday, too." "Well, not the same year," he said. He didn't understand what I thought was so funny.

There is another group we will be discussing and they are the opposite of the language delayed. Verbally astute, they are the charmers of the L.D. world. Often, they are super salesmen. One of our Achieve students sold more vacuum cleaners than anyone else in his state the year before he came to us. He admitted to charming his way through school. No one could bear to fail such a good-looking, friendly, helpful young man. That pretense of the continual charmer is hard to sustain all the time, and, although charm is a fine attribute, it won't work forever. If one is meeting someone briefly to sell a vacuum cleaner, charm may be the key, but working within a company requires sustained personal skills, both work related and social. These he did not have. However, while he was with us, he printed "I love Carbondale" bumper stickers and sold thousands; he's probably richer than I'll ever be. He graduated last year and I went to his wedding, but for a while there it was touch and go.

One way to classify people, in psychological terms, is as internal locus of control or external locus of control people. L.D. internal locus of control people tend to be highly verbal people who do a pretty good job of controlling their own lives, at least in some respects. L.D. external locus of control people often appear helpless and are much less verbally astute. Faced with a decision or the need to pay the light bill, they tend to try to find someone else to do it for them. As a group, they are less able to make friends and to get along in the world than are the internals.

INTERNAL LOCUS OF CONTROL
The Verbal Manipulators

"Hi, gorgeous!" Rob shouted down the hall when he saw me; I cringed a bit as other professors turned. Rob always greeted me that way and, although it was flattering, I believed him less than

I would have liked to because I knew him so well. Rob could charm anyone and get the person to do what he wanted, including me. It was a constant struggle not to be manipulated. He had a tendency to postpone until the last moment any assignment he was supposed to complete. One day, he dashed into the lab with a poorly constructed outline of a paper he was to hand in. Patti, his graduate assistant, was very worried but it was too late to teach him the correct method to use. Rob's comment was, "Not to worry. I'll just tell her I have a learning disability and it will be all right." Later, Patti fearfully asked what grade he had received, and he cheerfully reported, "B+, she loved it." Dumbfounded, Patti came to me and said, "What do you suppose he told the teacher a learning disability does to you for her to give him that grade?" No telling.

Later that semester, Rob's teacher called, very angry, and wanted to know if there was such a thing as a learning disability, and if there was, did he have it and if he did, what did it do to you? She had been manipulated once too often. We had to sit Rob down and help him understand what his constant manipulation of others could do, not only to himself but to other people with L.D. What would be the teacher's response to the next person with learning disabilities who requested her aid?

It is hard to give up behavior that has worked in the past when it is all one knows. Unable to impress others with their academic prowess, some of the learning disabled have learned to be manipulative to receive the positive feedback they desire and need.

Jon won everyone's heart at first meeting. Tall, handsome, and articulate, he depended on his charm to get what he needed. He admitted that he had graduated from high school on charm. One couldn't help but like him, he was so friendly and such fun to be with, but he absolutely would not do his work. He had not had to, indeed often could not, do his work before, so why should college be any different? Although we in the Achieve Program pressured him, driving out to his trailer to drag him out of bed, he simply would not study. The blow fell one morning when he came into the lab two hours before an algebra midterm exam and demanded that we teach him two months of algebra in two hours. We made a valiant attempt, but of course he failed the test. He was furious with us and disappeared for another month. At the end of that time, he came into the lab with a beautiful girl who was, he announced, all the help he needed. He firmly seated her at a typewriter and began to dictate. Academic probation finally convinced him that in the world beyond high school, one had to produce as well as be charming, and he began to allow us to teach him. Jon graduated a year ago, and I am very proud of him. He is still charming, but now he has knowledge to back up the charm.

Many of the internal locus of control students have as a first condition of academic achievement to get a girl, in their words, "who can type and spell." Jay had a unique way of accomplishing this goal. No sooner had he arrived on campus than he entered a male striptease contest at a local bar, billing himself as "Dr. Love." He won. Needless to say, he found many lovely young girls eager to do his work. I would like to explain to his mother why he is not coming in for all the tutoring sessions he is supposed to have, but that is not in my job description and besides, I'm a coward.

Even though the internal locus of control people are capable of handling the major and minor life issues with which we all must deal, that does not mean that they necessarily do it efficiently or with tact.

Sy was scheduled to take an exam at five o'clock. He is always very anxious before an exam but everything was ready. The test had arrived from the professor, his test proctor was waiting. Since it was after five, the office staff had gone home, except for a student worker who was responsible for making sure that everything proceeded efficiently.

When the worker told him to take the test in the lab, Sy lost his temper and shouted and yelled at her so violently that she thought he was about to strike her. She could supervise everything there, instead of running up and down the hall of the whole third floor. There was no one else around, it was nice and quiet. During the day when it is noisy and busy in the lab, students take their exams in private rooms at the other end of the hall, but that was not necessary at five o'clock. The mere suggestion of such a change made Sy react totally out of proportion as to the seriousness of the situation.

This type of irrational response is all too common, and most people stay as far away as they can from such behavior. They are fearful of what the person might do. I know Sy, and I know he really wouldn't hit her, but she didn't know that and I couldn't let him get away with it. He had to be told how others felt about his lack of control. He had to learn how others viewed him when he behaved that way. If he doesn't learn self-control, he won't last in an office very long.

EXTERNAL LOCUS OF CONTROL OR DO IT FOR ME

Those L.D. people who exhibit external locus of control behavior are much sadder individuals in my opinion than their internal counterparts, for they exhibit little control over their own lives. There are several possible reasons for this. Often, their families have done everything for them, even in instances where they could have easily managed for themselves. The unhappy results of this treatment are young adults who walk into my office with a light bill or an English assignment and expect me to take care of it for them. When I explain that I will show them how to do it but will not do it for them, they often become very angry because my suggesting that they do their own work is frightening since they have little faith in their abilities. Additionally, what could be simpler than getting someone else to do something for you that you don't want to bother with? "Hey, this life business sounds like work; what fun is that?" But the world has little respect for those perceived to be incapable, and so we must stand firm.

One of the first steps in this process is to expect the person with L.D. to be able to do his own work and to do it. He will often feel he cannot and is fearful even to try. Assure him of his ability to perform one specific act. Immediately sit down with him and take him through the steps necessary for success. Every little successful experience will make him more confident of his abilities and more willing to try the next step. Even such a thing as writing a check to pay for books is a fearful experience if one does not know how.

Analyze where the problem may lie and do something about it. Several Achieve students had expressed dismay at such simple tasks as buying their books. Coping mechanisms were interesting. One came to school with a checkwriter, which is a large cumbersome machine that would work all right for paying bills at home but could hardly be carried to the grocery store. Several used credit cards for every purchase they could; but grocery stores and the light company don't take credit cards. We eventually realized that the root of the problem was not the math involved, for one could always use a calculator, but the spelling! Not knowing how to spell twelve or twenty or the other written forms of numerals, they could not complete the checks. One student told me he could spell twenty, but not any of the teens, so he always shopped until he had twenty dollars worth of something. This is an efficient coping mechanism, but very hard on the budget. The verbally astute, internal people solved this spelling problem by having the store clerks fill out the check, claiming a sore wrist or hand, and looking pained all the while, but the external people were unable to do this. The problem was solved when we printed cards to be carried in a wallet with the written forms of numerals, i.e. thirty, fifty-five, and so forth, the spelling of the local establishments they were most likely to visit, months of the year and their numerical counterparts, and the names of the dormitories. These are handed out to all students at the beginning of the semester without comment. It was a simple solution, yet it gave them a tool that enabled them to be more in control of their own lives. We have not had a problem with check writing for several years now.

One of the advantages of working with a large group of people with L.D. is that one can begin to see what common problems exist. It is much more difficult to see the root of a problem when one is exposed to just one person or to a small class. In the spring, Southern Illinois University has a Springfest with something for everyone. There are bands, cardboard boat races, crafts, even jalapeno pepper eating contests. Yet, as my husband and I walked around, it struck me that many Achieve students whom I saw were alone; they were not participating in the activities, nor were they a part of a small group. Some joined us for a while before wandering off. They were spectators; spectators in a world from which they are often isolated because they do not understand the mechanisms of that world. It is a lonely existence for the externals.

In contrast, the internals were with others or working. One was selling soft drinks and as we went to buy one, saw us. Wanting to communicate but not wanting to identify himself as an Achieve member to those with whom he was working, he asked me how things were going at the club. I smiled and asked how he was getting along. "Fine," he said. He was still planning on getting through school on the five-year plan, meaning that he was staying with a reduced course load. No one, not even my husband, thought anything of our conversation, but the student and I had communicated fully. One might assume that that student is just more clever than the people who were alone, but such is not really the case. They are as clever as he, but he can work with people, he communicates well orally, he is more self-assured and comfortable with himself.

I am deeply troubled by parents' and educators' roles in developing our people into externals or internals. If the parent does everything for the child and tells him over and over how incapable he is, the end behavior is almost certain to be external, with the L.D. person unable to direct his own life. Teachers who do the work rather than teach it, or who constantly limit their students become part of the process.

Many of our students come into the university behaving as externals. Fortunately, through successful experiences, many develop into internals over the years, capable of directing their own lives. That is very hard for some parents to accept. Alice was offered a marvelous job opportunity in another state in her senior year. Her parents were appalled, having assumed that she would come back to live with them upon graduation. They really tried to sabotage the job opportunity, reminding her of what she had done when she was ten years old. She came to me in tears, telling me how much she appreciated her parents' efforts over the years, but that she couldn't go back home. It was too easy to fall back into the dependent role at home. "If I go back," she said, "I'll never get out." It took a lot of talking to convince her parents that the daughter they sent to school four years ago was not the same young woman today. Now she is a capable adult.

Female externals have an advantage over male externals in male-female relationships because society allows a female to stand back and let a man make a first approach. Females can be quiet and appear shy and still be accepted by acquaintances, at least for a while. Problems for them arise when a relationship with other girls or boys begins to show signs of developing further. Although eager for these relationships, often they cannot communicate well enough for relationships to really develop. Still, there are men who prefer a woman who takes little action on her own, who like a woman who will allow them to direct her life, and so in a rather sad way, because we may never know her true potential, she has an advantage. During the 1984 presidential election campaign, a gentleman said to me, "I see that the three wives will be in the area tomorrow; Joan Mondale is here, and Nancy Reagan is there, and Geraldine Ferraro. . . ." I answered, "No, that's two wives and one potential vice-president!" Sad, but still a common attitude.

Many L.D. people seem extremely self-centered. This self-centeredness is a real problem because when they spend so much time thinking about how they feel, or what others are thinking about them, there is very little left over for thinking or caring about others. Because they have had to be constantly concerned about how they are appearing to others, they often fail to listen, jumping into conversations inappropriately. People do not enjoy being around those who think and talk only about themselves. Although we can understand clearly how such situations develop and why, understanding is not treatment, and treatment is the key.

We absolutely must teach these skills so that they are no longer barriers to socialization. Just as Sy had to learn how his behavior appeared to others, so we must address any behavior that appears abnormal to others, for that is what will keep them lonely.

4 I'M TIRED OF BEING SOLOMON
PARENTING—THE CRITICAL COMPONENT

It is a sad cliché that having a handicapped child too often results in a handicapped family. A handicapped family is one that does not function as well as it might, due to emotional factors caused by the handicapped child's condition. These emotions have not been resolved to the point where they can get on with the business of living. Instead of seeing the handicap as only one small part of the child, the handicap is all that some parents see.

It is not easy. Nobody wants to give birth to a handicapped child, nobody actively seeks the pain that goes with being different. Parents feel pain, frustration, fear, and guilt when they discover they have a handicapped child.

Often, one of the first questions parents ask when they discover that their child is learning disabled is, "What was the cause?" Also implied is, "Am I somehow to blame?" Perhaps that was your question, too. Because people expect, subconsciously at least, punishment for their sins, parents sometimes feel that such a child is God's punishment, especially if the child was unwanted. All of us have within us feelings of inadequacy; parents wonder if this problem is in some way related to something they have done or not done. They feel this way, in part, because we have schools which teach us how to be teachers or lawyers, but no one ever thought to teach us how to be parents. One has to pass a test to drive a car, but there is no required test for parenthood. A baby is born or adopted, and suddenly parents are thrust into a role for which neither training nor experience has prepared them. Parents are not very sure of themselves, they know they make mistakes, and, with the firstborn in particular, they are insecure.

Now they are parents, expected to know how to handle all of those situations from birth through adulthood.

Usually the only frame of reference parents have is how they themselves were raised. We all remember how we were treated by our parents; when they spanked us, what we got away with. Some of us came from loving, caring homes where we felt loved and cherished at least most of the time. Others of us vowed we would never raise our children the way we were raised. Most of us do, however; we know no other way. We even catch ourselves saying the same things our parents said to us, something we swore we'd never do.

Sometimes parents are tired and cross, impatient when they know they should not be. They see other mothers who seem to bake cookies with their children every day, whose homes are always neat, and whose children always behave, while they never get the ironing done and their child is hyperactive. No wonder they feel insecure.

We all wish we were more patient or better listeners. We are cross and tired at times, speaking sharply when we wish we had spoken calmly. When a teenager says, "Everyone else is allowed to," parents wonder if they are too strict or not strict enough. Sometimes they even feel jealous or maligned. Why does life seem so simple for some people, while they have a school conference nearly every week and hardly ever hear anything good about this child they love? Maybe they are angry. They never did anything to deserve this, so why should it happen to them? What did they do wrong?

These are perfectly natural feelings. Everyone has them, not just those who have learning disabled children. Those of us who have children with problems sometimes allow our feelings to get in the way of our ability to cope with life, a position we must guard against. Getting our own feelings under control is often the biggest problem we face.

Sometimes we already have problems at home, and the knowledge that we have a handicapped child only serves to compound these difficulties. Often, the area of disagreement between husband and wife is over the special child and how to handle him. Fathers are not with their children as much as mothers are and often find it difficult to understand the mother's concern. Usually, because most school conferences are held during the day, fathers cannot attend, and it is the mother who has to sit and listen to teachers relate the difficulties the child is having. Most of what fathers hear is secondhand. Solutions sometimes seem simple to him—more discipline, watch the child more closely, be more strict—and he doesn't realize that these are not necessarily solutions for the special child. He is working hard all day; why must he come home to hear how his wife can't handle a little child? Mother then retaliates from this attack upon her child rearing abilities, "If you were ever home," "If you ever played with him," and so forth. Everyone is miserable, especially the child, because he knows they are arguing about him again.

For most parents, the knowledge of the child's disability may have been only a faint suspicion before he entered school. How alert they were depends on several factors: whether they had older children to whom they could compare him; the nature of his disability—hyperactivity and speech problems are easier to detect, for instance, than potential learning problems; and how helpful their pediatricians were. For some parents, the first call from the school is a surprise, for others it is a confirmation of their worst fears.

The conference at school is usually held with a school psychologist or a learning disability specialist, and suddenly parents are hearing about a condition they never knew existed, hearing terms they don't understand. In a little while they go home, grateful perhaps, that at last something will be done, but confused nonetheless. If both parents were present, discussion is easier, but usually it's the mother giving the father secondhand information again, much of which she may not understand herself.

Sometimes the diagnosis comes as a relief, because the fears are often worse than the reality. One father listened very carefully as I discussed his child, then asked if it "ran in families." I said, yes, it sometimes appeared to, and he stated, "Thank God.

All these years I thought I was stupid." But for many parents, such a diagnosis seems like a disaster. The questions families ask revolve around valid concerns: "Will my child ever be able to support himself? What will happen to him when we are gone?" For parents of both sexes, the label "handicapped" may seem like the end of a dream.

In general, the mothers seem to accept the diagnosis more readily than most fathers are able to. They have usually spent more time with the child, they have sensed something was wrong and are thus more prepared.

Egos are at stake. Many parents feel that their children's successes are reflections of their own abilities. They sometimes use their children's achievements to enhance their own stature in the eyes of co-workers and friends. When the man's boss is relating a story about his son, the football star, and his child can't even catch a ball, about whom does he become frustrated? The child, that's who. Oh, he doesn't come home and yell, "Why aren't you a football hero?" but he feels frustrated just the same. Before L.D. children have remediation, some of them don't excel in anything, and that can be hard to take for a parent, particularly if the parent is an achiever himself.

Each family has its own set of value judgments, and we want our children to excel in areas that are important to us. In my family, academic honors are important. That is our value system. We are not too concerned with sports, but achievement academically and an interest in the arts are necessities. My elder son, however, is a sports fan; any sport intrigues him and he enjoys participating and observing them. Fortunately, he excels in the areas that are important to me also. If he were a sports fan only, we would probably have some problems, because my value system would be in conflict with his. The same kind of value conflict is almost certainly present in your home, in some form or other. I cannot give you a perfect plan to ameliorate the situation because I haven't discovered it myself, but I can ask you to be aware of it and to think about whether or not it is fair to insist that the drummer you listen to be the same one that your child must also heed.

After having admitted that we are human, with all of the frailties and strengths that admission includes, it helps to examine our reactions.

The controlled rage parents often feel at the school system, at their spouse, even at their child, the total unfairness of it all, needs to be identified and dealt with. It is real. It is understandable, it is normal. Often, there are several stages parents have to go through in the acceptance of the child's disability. The first is denial that there is anything wrong. Minds and hearts want to reject such an awful idea. After that stage comes a mourning period, for at the time they do not know the implications of the disability for the rest of his life; they wonder what will become of him, and of themselves. Other stages follow: anger, fear, frustration, guilt, and acceptance, not necessarily in that order. To go through each of these stages is normal; to stay at one stage, instead of growing through it, further handicaps the child and the family. How long the parents remain in a stage (and they may be in several at the same time) depends on factors of family situation, available resources, support from the school system, severity of the disability, and their own personalities. The responses are as different as night and day. Consider three families, all in the same school system. One family said: "Well, poor child, we'll simply love him as he is." Another took their son to faith healers, hair analyzers, and eye-tracking experts. I never could understand how they found so many "experts." The third family said: "Okay, he has a learning disability, he's still a great kid. How do we help him?"

The problem with the first response is that it comes from a basis of pity, and pity does not help anyone grow. It is a truism that if we expect nothing from people, we usually get nothing. People have a way of living up to, or down to, our expectations. The second family was not content to give the child the remedial help he needed and support him during that time; they wanted an immediate cure, and there is none. What they did succeed in doing was to teach the child, by their tremendous overconcern, that he was indeed very different, and that they were desperate for him not to be. This negative reaction did not help his self-confidence. The third family looked at the disability as only a small part of their child. There were things about him which were likable; he was a worthwhile individual. So he had a learning disability, they would help him and find others to help him. In the meantime, he felt secure and loved.

The importance of parents' responses to the disability cannot be overemphasized because it so deeply affects the child's perception of himself. If the emphasis is only on the disability instead of the whole child, seeing himself through his parents' eyes, he will see only the disability. Parents need to help him see the whole of his being; they can only do that by looking for it themselves.

Once parents get into the acceptance stage, they can begin to take effective action and thereby assure a productive life for their child. There are many help stations along the way. Parent support groups, or L.D. adult groups if their child is older, are the most effective ways of dealing with these feelings, but sometimes therapy by a trained clinician makes a world of difference.

School systems are not uniformly wise, and parents may not always agree with them. Parents must learn to ask questions and accept only what seems reasonable to them. It is important to remember that no one knows the child as the parents do. No one else sees him as he wakes in the morning or goes to bed at night. No one else knows his moods or what makes him happy. No one else loves him as much or cares about him in the ways that his parents do. They are his best friends; the persons he wants most to please and the ones who must ease his way into that adult world.

Although it is the parents' responsibility to guide him, they often hesitate to do as much as they should. They have seen their L.D. child injured so often that their stomachs hurt at the remembrance of that pain. Each of us has our own set of "horror" stories. It is even more natural, then, for parents to want to avoid any more pain for their children by reminding them of their faults. The tricky part is the need to lead them in the paths parents know they need to follow, while protecting their already

, requiring judgment parents
ed to say to my husband, "I'm
h all his wisdom. I want to be
ry I was not allowed. Neither

ldren. In addition to not want-
ten become immune to behav-
r nonhandicapped children. A
en her daughter and her L.D.
er to the back of the station
e her, at which point her son
! I never get in trouble!" His
, although she may have an
led one, and vowed never to
oman.
nilies education is still valued
a family where the son is a
bright, fine boy who has learning disabilities. He excels in math
and sports. His younger sister is just one of those brilliant little
girls who adores anything academic. One would think that each
child could be valued for his own accomplishments, but such is not
the case. The girl's accomplishments are constantly downgraded
to make the boy feel better. These are bright, well-educated parents but I tremble at the messages they are giving their children.
A father of one of my students said, "Tim is not like our smart
children." I fairly shouted, "Tim is one of your smart children!"
Tim graduated this spring. I hope his father has changed his mind.

THE FATHER'S ROLE

There are some fathers who take an active role in their children's
development, but they are few. Caught up in the role of breadwin-
ner, probably raised in an atmosphere where nurturing was the
mother's role, most fathers tend to have less impact on the up-

bringing of the children than do the mothers. A father often finds it very difficult to accept that this child he loves has a disability. Many fathers feel that their sons are extensions of themselves; some even say that a child is their immortality. Sometimes, even before the child was born, fathers have thought about how much better this child will be than his father. He will go to the best schools, be a football star, adding all the dreams of a lifetime to the hopes of the future. This is especially true if the father is not really happy with his life. He wants something better for his son. The fact that the child is an individual, not a small prototype of his dad, comes as a shock to some fathers. If the father had learning disabilities, he probably went untreated and he may have experienced the same kind of pain his child now feels. If so, there may be some empathy and understanding. Many, though, have become successful adults and feel that the child, and later the adult, should do as he did and grow up and produce. Indeed, if whatever support was needed was somehow available, in the hyperactive in particular, the tendency is to become a successful businessman. Those very problems of overactivity, perseveration, boundless energy, are the same qualities which produce the most prominent of businessmen. They do not produce successful children.

When the father is less successful, there may be a denial of the child's problem because it is too painful to remember one's own experiences. If the father has taken on the macho image, to have a son who is not a football star may be a disappointment. However, when parents say to me that they have never been able to be proud of their children, then I have to ask, "In what activities have you involved him so that you, and he, could be proud of some accomplishment?"

Sometimes the blame is placed on the mother, "If you were home more," if she is working, or "If you didn't baby him so much," if she's not. It is a situation where no one wins, especially the person with L.D.

Finally, there is denial. "This is my kid. There can't be anything wrong with him. Teachers just don't know how to teach anymore."

As far as fathers are concerned, most L.D. girls have a much easier life than boys in the years before adulthood, for they are often excused for their behavior. After all, mothers are supposed to teach girls the skills they need, and they can always get married. The results, of course, are children in adult bodies, wanting all the things an adult wants without the slightest idea of how to attain them. They enter the adult world hesitantly, flying back to the parental home at the first sign of stress.

I remember when Sara's parents brought her to school. Her father's question was, "What should Sara do on Saturday night?" We literally had to make a list; she could go to a movie with her roommate, she could watch television, and so on. Sara's behavior was so immature that it was difficult not to respond to her at that level. On Monday morning, Sara appeared at our door and announced brightly, "I'm ready to go to school now!" Without thinking, Sally answered, "Very good, Sara!" Later Sally said to me, "Dr. C., I responded as if I were back teaching fifth grade!" In a way, she was. The socially more astute students are adept at spotting such behavior as Sara's and resent it. One of the guys in the Achieve Program said, "Do you realize what a reflection her behavior is on the rest of us?" Even among the learning disabled, she is somewhat rejected.

I have often said that many of the socially disabled girls have to be pushed, kicking and screaming all the way, into adulthood; but not to push, not to demand that they become all that they can be, is to assure that they will not lead independent lives of their own. Some, desperate for boyfriends and needing love, become sexually active, but most just stay home.

I have mentioned before the impact of others outside the home on the emerging adolescent and adult and such influences are indeed important, but of far more importance is the family unit and the interactions within that unit.

Parents do not unanimously like their children, particularly those parents who have to deal with a hyperactive, destructive, willful child. They often hate to go home, to face again a home which is in constant turmoil.

For many parents, the responsibility of taking care of a child who is constantly doing something that is disruptive to family life is overwhelming, and so it is not hard to understand why parents who may love their child at some level do not really like him. I tried to get Brian's family to consider giving him a pet, something for which he was responsible and which would give him love and acceptance. Brian's dad, too bitter to understand, suggested a boa constrictor. Brian was five years old. That hurt me, for I cared what happened to that family, but in all honesty I did not have to go home with Brian. I did not have to lock each door, hide each knife and lighter. I could do other things besides just watch Brian, but somebody had to. Usually it's the mother, as too often the father leaves the problem to her. I have directed parent groups to help people deal with their handicapped youngsters for over fifteen years. Although it is getting better, in general only the mothers attend.

THE MOTHER'S ROLE

As a group, mothers of learning disabled children spend more time involved with the education and daily lives of their children than do fathers. They are more likely to spot, and be worried about, those early clues that this child is somehow different, and they are more likely to be ridiculed for those concerns. I remember taking my two-year-old son, my third child, to the pediatrician saying, "This child is different. He rarely cries when he falls down and it seems to me his speech development is slow," only to be told that I was an overprotective mother. Two more years of not understanding why my tactilely defensive child hated to wear ironed and starched church clothes, or why he was so afraid of his space suit costume, were to go by before he was diagnosed.

Tactilely defensive children are physically bothered by any stiff clothing, such as blue jeans, and want to wear the softest item of clothing available. A mother told me that her son liked hand-me-down clothes best of all, because they were very soft and had "holes just where I like them!"

Lance wouldn't wear his space suit, a cute Halloween costume, because he was afraid he would be sent up in a space capsule, since we lived at Cape Kennedy at the time. I didn't understand and he did not have the language to explain. When I understood that these and other things were related to his learning disability, I had to deal with that most prevalent of maternal feelings: guilt. So I, like others, learned I had sometimes punished him for things he could not help, spilling the milk or hiding his church clothes. I felt so guilty.

A mother has dreams, too, and although they may not be identical to those of the father, they are just as important to her. Often her ego is entwined with the child's behavior and abilities. One has only to listen to a discussion among mothers of when various babies learned to walk or talk to realize how true this assertion is. It is she who bears the brunt of the comments if her child does not behave properly; it is a direct reflection on her abilities as a wife and mother. If she stays at home all the time with her children and has no outside interests, she may live only through their achievements. Nobody gives bonuses for clean ovens, and often the only reinforcement she receives is when others say, "How well behaved your children are!" Her own opinion of herself is enhanced or diminished by the comments others make. Many women feel that the most important job they have is that of being a good wife and mother. I feel that way myself. The other things I do are like icing on the cake—exciting, self-fulfilling, but not essential. If I fail as a wife and mother, I fail in the area most important to me, that is why it has the ability to hurt me so much if I feel I am not doing a good job.

But, there is a danger if we allow our desires to be supermoms to govern our lives. If we are so stereotyped that being a super-mom is all we care about, we sometimes resent the interference of anyone else, even our own husbands. Our homes become little kingdoms where we rule as queens and any disagreement with the way we are handling things becomes an attack upon the citadel.

Psychology has not helped either. A great deal of literature has been written that blames virtually everything on Mom, from autism to homosexuality. Now, fortunately, research is looking at these problems in a different light. Lauretta Bender, a specialist in this field, has said that what was once criticized as a need in the mother to encourage dependency in her child, is now being understood as a response in the mother to the very real need of the child. Most learning disabled children do not seem to develop a consistency in their crying patterns as soon as other babies do. As a result, mothers cannot understand as easily what the baby wants. These and other problems often make mothering of these infants difficult and frustrating. To be told it's your fault as well may seem to be the proverbial straw on the camel's back.

A friend of mine who had three learning disabled sons had been living with guilt for ten years because a psychiatrist had told her that she was a terrible mother and that was why her sons had learning problems. When professionals finally began to recognize the symptomology and her sons were properly evaluated, she was asked how she had managed to keep them so emotionally stable when their problems were so severe! Her gratitude was immense, of course, but she was angry about those agonizing ten years of doubt and frustration when, confused about her own abilities, she had tried to help her sons. "Your child has a learning problem, Mrs. Jones. Leave him at home and you and your husband come in for therapy," was too often the only solution offered. Fortunately, it happens much more rarely now.

If her husband thinks there is nothing wrong with the child, there is usually no outlet for those hidden, nagging voices of concern. To whom can she talk? When she gets together with friends for coffee or visits her mom, she wants her child to be brighter and healthier than her neighbor's or her sister's children, not handicapped. In our society, producing a less-than-perfect child is often perceived as a defect in us, his parents. It is not a comfortable role.

It is usually the mother who has to attend the teacher conferences where the news is often bad, and she must supervise the birthday party which no one wanted to attend. Mothers carry these memories throughout their lives. A mother of a twenty-five-year-old related to me an incident which had happened with her daughter when she was in grade school. As her daughter was leaving for school, she said to her, "Kelly Sue, you look very pretty today," to which her daughter replied, "Mom, just pray I get through recess." For fifteen years, she has remembered. Each mother has her own memories, which can be a painful burden, so all of us have several things with which to deal. When my son and daughter were growing up, there was a popular song called "You and Me Against the World," and that is exactly how I felt. You parents probably do, too. It is not easy to feel so alone, your parenting skills questioned, your beloved child hurting.

The major roles of disciplining and much of the educational load falls upon the mother as well. Helping with homework every night when she might like to watch television, too, can be a dreadful chore. She has the right to be tired, the right to some time to herself; rarely does she get it. This problem can build up resentment of the father and sometimes of the L.D. child, as well. Besides, tutoring can be terribly unrewarding, since the child flunked the spelling test anyway. When parents and teachers don't understand that what the child knows tonight he may not know tomorrow, confusion and anger arise, and it becomes very easy to get very frustrated with the child.

Mothers have the most difficult of roles, and their own feelings about the learning disabled person may be colored by how much support they get from their husbands, other family members, and school personnel. They are often torn between the need to work with their L.D. children and the need to nurture their other children. If she is a working mother, time is already precious; if she is a single parent, the situation is even worse. Take heart, though. Those years we spent at the dining room table turned my son into a programmed learner. He learned that he had to put aside what he wanted to do until the homework was completed. It has been a valuable lesson for his university work and I never had to chide him about studying, but at the time we were both exhausted.

Judy Pelletier, executive director of the Atlantic Conference on Learning Disabilities, said it so beautifully in a letter to me, "Mothers are not a renewable resource. Further, their individual lifestyles do not give each of them the same mothering qualities—all patient, all alert, all selfless, all child-oriented, all devotion—in supply to last forever. Mothers are just apt to ask, if only in a whisper, 'What about me?'"

DEVELOPING SOLUTIONS

What, then, are the solutions? The most important message to convey to any child, however old he is, is that he is loved just as he is, which doesn't mean one has to like all his behavior. It has been said that in order to give love to others, you first have to like and love yourself. So much unhappiness occurs because our children don't like themselves. Love can't, or shouldn't, be withheld because someone can't do something well. Love must be freely given, no matter what the disablility is. But remember the parents who said, "Well, we will just take him home and love him." Just love him! What happened to tough love, to active parental involvement? What happened to helping him grow?

On the other hand, professionals may give parents such advice. After my son's diagnosis I was told to "take him home and love him" because there was no one within a hundred miles who was trained to help him. I was not impressed. I already loved him and I had every intention of taking him home! I wanted help and I wanted it now. I wrote letters to all types of professionals and the next month flew to my first learning disabilities convention. Listening, taping, and taking copious notes, I accosted people whom

I had heard in the halls, even at breakfast, saying, "Excuse me, but I have this child. . . ." Mercifully, they were almost universally kind and caring. In my own professional life, I have tried to emulate what they gave me and respond in kind to other searching parents. I remember how I felt.

At the time, although I always loved Lance, I sometimes grew angry and frustrated too. We spent more time in the emergency room than all of my other children combined. He stuck a piece of popcorn up his nose once. Years later when he had the verbal skills to explain it to me, he said, "Well, you can breathe through your nose and mouth, and you eat with your mouth; I wanted to see if you could eat with your nose, too." Perfectly logical.

All children must have love and help. I think that one of the saddest findings about L.D. is that some parents expect less of their children than either the teachers or the persons with L.D. do of themselves.

As parents or teachers, we need to be extremely aware of the hidden messages we give children, for hidden messages can be as clear to the child as are those which are stated clearly. We must make certain that they know we believe in them, and our actions must fit our words. Unthinkingly, we give hidden messages all the time.

Every evening, Andrea's father took a few bricks from the construction site of the new house across the street. By the time the new house was built, he had a new patio, but when Andrea came home with a toy she'd taken from the store, she was punished. Message: It's all right for Daddy to take what he wants, but it's not all right for you to.

Sharon did not want to talk to Ruth and told her daughter to tell Ruth that she was not at home. Message: It's okay to lie if you don't want to do something or if it's not convenient.

Walter bragged about how much he had saved on his income taxes by manipulating some figures. He was very upset when his son was caught cheating on his economics exam, and wondered how he could have produced such a son.

A mother and father and their six-year-old son sat in the room with me. The mother was relating her problems in school and both parents laughed as she told how she had rebelled against the school's authority. They were there to see me because of their concern over their son, who would not mind his teacher.

It seems to me that many parents assume that their children develop a unique form of deafness and hear only what their parents want them to hear, for they relate such incidents in the child's presence and then are appalled when the child does what the parent has done.

Sometimes parents feel despair at the problems their children face daily. A good treatment for despair is to get busy. Action, the feeling that you are doing something about the problem, can be therapeutic. However, because of their children's problems, most parents have had to fight long and hard for services. That makes it more difficult for many to lessen control over their children as they grow up. Some parents almost seem to fear a loss of control over their children and feel that if they are not right there all the time, the child will immediately get into trouble. So it is with many of my college students. Sometimes, because of past behavior and the students' new-found freedom, such concern is justified, but at some point in their lives we have to let them go.

I sadly remember Robert. He was a good, down-to-earth boy from a rural area. Robert would have been okay if his mother had just left him some degree of self-respect, for he did nothing bad. Still, she called him every Saturday night to be certain he was home and had someone call her every Sunday to be sure he'd gone to church. He knew his mother didn't trust him at all. The saddest part was that he really was a delightful young man who had never been in any trouble.

I wrote to her about him, because the constant pressure was causing him serious emotional distress and he was doing nothing of which she would not approve. She wrote back saying that others could sometimes see good in children that parents couldn't see. There was nothing I could do.

Robert left school and went far away where his mother couldn't find him. He has no skills, and no higher education. Tell me, is he better off?

Irv, in contrast, came from a large metropolitan community. When the family visited, he kept his chin on his chest and offered no comment, while his mother went through every paper and educational intervention he had ever had. His father slept. I got the impression the father had heard this too many times before. After a while, I wished I could just go to sleep also.

The real loser was Irv. After he had been with us for a couple of months, his head began to come up; he was beginning to smile and to make some decent grades. He began to develop some friendships, but the friends, his mother said, were never good enough for him. His mother really could not stand not to be needed, and she began to undermine his success. She would arrive from 250 miles away promptly every Thursday afternoon and leave on Monday, every week. We tried to fight for him, but without success. He's where she wants him now, at home with no skills and little future.

Parents must examine their own fears, goals, and behavior to determine if they really have their child's future in mind. My heart still hurts for Irv.

Just as parents and teachers can demand too little, so they can demand too much. Gary was a very bright young man whose father was never satisfied. Gary received scant praise and was constantly pressured to do better, do it right, *ad infinitum.* I was worried about him and told his father so. His father finally quit pushing him so hard the day that Gary lost control and squeezed his father's head between his hands as hard as he could. Gary couldn't stand it anymore. Everyone has to feel good about himself some of the time.

In Joe's case, both of his parents were unforgiving, his mother perhaps even more so than his father. I never saw them when they weren't cross. Constantly pressured to get better grades, study more, have less free time, put out more effort, Joe had learned that the only way to survive was to be totally agreeable with everyone. Now twenty years old, he will try to do exactly what he is told, with a smile. He never has a problem; everything is always wonderful; all of his classes are marvelous; everything is just fine. It isn't, of course; when he flunks tests he won't tell those who are trying to help him. Everything is bottled up inside him. It is terribly sad never to be able to please those whom you love. I know this pseudo Joe very well, and I try to help his parents understand what they are doing, to little avail, it seems, but I keep wondering where the real Joe is. I do not think I have met him yet. I hope someday I will.

Not all L.D. people are nice to be around, just as not all blind or physically impaired or nonhandicapped people are nice to be around. No parent wants to feel that he doesn't particularly like his child; parents are supposed to like their kids, and when they don't, tremendous feelings of guilt well up inside, but the truth is, some children can be unpleasant. As one father said to me: "Her idea of independence is anarchy." He was right, it was.

Parents must try to respond to irritability with calmness and humor. I used to say to a particularly cross teenage son or daughter, "My, your hormones must really be active this morning. I hope they calm down soon." Sometimes they were cross because of an upcoming test or quiz. I learned that dispositions improved when I made them pills out of colored bread dough sprinkled with a little sugar, and on the day of the test, popped a "courage" pill into their mouths on their way out the door. The pill said to them, "I understand what you're going through and I'm on your side." It seemed to help. My father still reminds me, and questions my mental health over the blue or pink mashed potatoes I used to sometimes serve, but I found that such things delighted the children and took the edge off a bad day. I also taught them the primary colors of red, blue, and yellow, and how they combined to form the secondary colors of purple, green, and orange through bread dough and potatoes. I admit that sometimes my husband groaned.

Until they are helped, many L.D. people tend to be extremely self-centered. They do not seem to understand others' feelings as well as they should, so there is little sympathy for another's feelings or emotional state. This is a good reason for sharing with them how we are feeling, remembering that our body language or facial expression may have very little meaning to them. As a result, L.D. people can seem insensitive when they are really unaware of our emotional states.

As a teacher, I have worked with many L.D. people who were not particularly pleasant, whom I did not enjoy seeing as they came through the door, but as I have taught my graduate students, "You don't have to love them, you have to teach them; if you later come to love them, and they you, that is the frosting on the cake." And invariably, this is what happens. As the problems of the L.D. student are dealt with, he begins to see others' needs in positive ways. He begins to seek out ways to help and in so doing, he becomes a more pleasant and likable person. The steps they follow are small and hesitant, but each represents growth. I fondly remember Jim, a particularly abrasive young man when he first joined us. I knew Jim was developing in these ways one day when I was walking across campus, uncovered, in a gentle rain, which I rather enjoyed. Jim raced to my side and held his notebook over my hair so it wouldn't get wet. It was his first step in showing he cared about me, a hesitant step out of himself.

Finally, we need to analyze ourselves, the messages we are communicating, the memories we are building. What are your best memories? I remember a Valentine my father made for me when I was about nine; I remember the Santa Claus he painted on my little table; I remember the perfect fairy costume my mother made for me one Halloween.

What will my children remember about me? They say they remember me taking off work to take the injured squirrel to the veterinarian; sitting for hours painting the internal organs of the Invisible Man model so Lance could study body structures. These are some of our memories. Interestingly, not an important memory, mine or theirs, is about schoolwork.

Don is an incredible young man, so insightful at times that I am overwhelmed by his ability to get to the heart of things. We were talking about his efforts at overcoming his disabilities and I talked about Lance, whom he knew well. Don said, "I just can't believe he has a learning disability." "Oh," I said, "listen to what happened over Thanksgiving," and related an instance where Lance's auditory receptive disabilities had been revealed. But Don shook his head and said, "The difference between Lance and me is that he wasn't raised handicapped." Remember that. Don is so right; if we raise them to feel they are handicapped, they will be. If parents and teachers help them to feel good about themselves, they can face the rest of life, with problems, yes, but none they can't handle.

We can never emphasize the love we share too often. Some parents seem to really talk to their children only when the child has done something wrong. Communication in any relationship has to be built and constantly worked on. As parents, these are the steps we must follow: leading, directing, pushing, and sometimes shoving, if need be, but always with love and a deep, abiding faith that there are qualities the world will cherish in our L.D. children.

5

SCORE: SON 1, GINOTT 0
WHAT ONE FAMILY LEARNED

When my son was growing up, I bought "Between Parent and Child" by Haim Ginott, and read it faithfully. In the book were interchanges which a parent was to use with his child. It went like this:

Son: I don't like broccoli. I hate it!
Me: You're angry that I served broccoli today.
Son: No, I'm not angry. I just won't eat it.
Score: Son 1, Ginott 0.

It went on like that until finally one day I said, "Look, you're not answering the way you are supposed to."

Son: Huh?
Me: The book says that when I say, "You're angry," you are
supposed to answer . . .
Son: What book?
Me: This book. See, it says right here that this is what you are
supposed to say.
Son: Are you trying to program me from a book?

By this time, indignant though we both were, we were laughing. Humor was one of the keystones to our survival, and that is an important point.

Parents and teachers need to try to find humor in situations. It was often difficult to find humor in what was happening to us, but we tried; and so often what could have been traumatic turned out to be not quite so bad after all. When Lance flunked the spelling test, I would tease him about the gorgeous secretary he was going to have. When he was feeling bad about some failure, I'd organize an activity that he really liked, such as making plaster of paris casts of animal footprints in the woods, and then tease him about my life as Tarzan's mother.

When Lance was very young, I used to have him cover one eye and practice placing one of his sister's plastic bracelets over the necks of soda bottles to increase hand-eye coordination. We did this for many months. When he was in high school, he won in several categories at the science fair and came home with his prizes. I hugged him with such joy and said, "Wow, honey. Things certainly have changed, haven't they?" He looked down and quietly said, "Yes, they have. When I was in second grade, I used to pray that God would let me die, because there wasn't anything I could do well." I burst into tears and said, "Oh, darling. I'm so sorry you had to go through all that. I was working as hard as I knew how to help you." And he said, "That's all right, Mom. The only thing that got me through was you, and knowing that I was the best bracelet-putter-on-soda-bottles in the whole neighborhood." When he graduated in premed, I lost all decorum and cheered and cried as he received his degree, for only he and I really understood the cost. We had survived.

L.D. must be kept in perspective. Although it seemed overwhelming at times, we learned to treat it as what it is—a small part of the individual—and to involve the kids in all sorts of activities. Over the years, my children took classes in everything the park district, the "Y," and the community had to offer. They learned the trampoline (good for position in space and developing body control), and horseback riding (Tara learned her right side from her left from that activity. [I told her the horse would kick her if she tried to get on from the wrong side—a fact, but also quite a motivator.]). Swimming involved bilateral movement using both sides of the body; canoeing, fishing, and science projects each taught them something. We built a hot air balloon and blew it up with a hair dryer; for weeks I had a baby shark in the refrigerator and a microscope on the dining room table. In our house, if you cut yourself you couldn't treat it until you bled on a slide!

How did these and many other activities help them? First, it exposed them to a variety of pursuits, some of which they learned they could do well. Second, they were doing something not everyone could do, so they had something to talk about to others, which set them apart in positive rather than negative ways for a change. Third, they learned that there is a whole lot more to this world than reading, math, and spelling. Fourth, they learned to organize. One can't collect blood samples or stamps or compile a bird list without organization, and of course one never knows what interests will carry over into adult life. Ballet dancing didn't; Tara is 5 feet 10 inches tall. But, the bird watching we did to help her eyes focus together and to increase visual perceptual skills piqued an interest in both of us which continues to this day. I'm president of our Audubon Society chapter; we call her room the "Wild Kingdom," and she would like to be a veterinarian. The microscope on the table continued to intrigue Lance, who is now in medical school. Of course, he also broke his leg horseback riding. Well, you can't win them all! However, Tara is a terrific rider and Lance passed the course for Life Guard. Photography is a good choice; it can be done alone or shared with others. There is a finished product that rather speaks for itself and is a starting point for conversation. In her senior year of high school, Tara became the official school photographer. Of course, our bathroom became a darkroom, story of my life, but all the football players were friendly because they wanted their pictures taken, and it didn't matter if she had someone to go to the game with because she had a place, she belonged.

Such things can backfire, of course, and in our house they often did, as with the darkroom. I find that people with learning disabilities are very attracted to animals, particularly the babies or the weak. Perhaps they sense the vulnerability of the little ones and sympathize. On the other hand, animals are nonjudgmental. They don't care how you did on the spelling test or whether you caught the ball. They are always there when you need to be comforted. They don't get mad at you and they love you when you don't think anyone else does. Animals can fill a void.

While I understand and value this quality, I was sometimes sorry there wasn't more of a void in our home, since it always seemed to be overflowing with animals of some type. I won once. Lance asked if he could have a snake and I drew the line. I told him he could have a snake or he could have a mother; he could not have both. Since a mother cooked dinner and found your toys, I guess I sounded like the better deal.

Tara was more subtle. Her favorite trick was to wait until I had settled in with a martini and the paper, both of which I richly deserved, and plop some small, adorable, furry baby in my lap. Her theory was that once I held it, rabbit, guinea pig, kitten, hamster, etc., it was as good as home. That was usually the case, but there was always excellent *rationale* to bolster the cases. For instance, I never knew before Tara told me, that rabbits are used to warm green houses and that therefore, logically, all our heating bills would go down, and if one rabbit was good, obviously three would be even better. If one adds guinea pigs, hamsters—the list is formidable—why, before you knew it the electric company would owe us money! Nobody ever mentioned summer.

Children's limits are often only those we place upon them. There is more to life than school and we must find ways to help them feel good about themselves. Teachers should take the time to learn the interests of their L.D. students and devise a way for their interests to be shared with the class. Success in one thing builds confidence and fosters success in other areas, and anyway, how long has it been since someone asked you your reading level? Put L.D. where it belongs.

We learned to teach the rules of polite behavior; to stand when someone enters the room; to stick out one's hand in a firm handshake, to teach a handshake; to maintain eye contact and nod once in a while when someone is talking to you. I have spoken at length elsewhere about maintaining eye contact because it is so important in such things as job interviews. A father and son came to be interviewed for the Achieve Program. Every time he thought I wasn't looking, the father would lightly tap his son and whisper, "Eye contact! Eye contact!" Ah, well.

We learned to teach our children how to answer the telephone and how to take messages. We put up a permanent message board with 'Who? What? When? and Where?' near the phone and taught them how to fill in the blanks. We role played: "Hello," or "Smith's residence," "Yes, she is, just a moment please," and insisted that they answer that way.

We learned to teach them to organize and tried to temper discipline with humor. I thought my daughter's room would drive me mad. It was so cluttered that when the hamster escaped we couldn't find him for hours. I put up signs: "Keep America Beautiful, Clean Your Room," and "Condemned by the Board of Health: No One May Enter This Room Unless She Has Been Innoculated Against Cholera, Malaria, and Yellow Fever," "Stop! Enter At Your Own Risk. We Have Lost 2 Cats In This Room. You May Be Next!" She put up a sign: "Mothers Keep Out." This wasn't working.

You can be smarter than I was. Get a series of boxes for his room or your classroom and label them with pictures if he is young, or with words if he reads adequately. Often, L.D. children simply do not know where to start a task, so structuring a task is the first step. "Pick up all of the cars; they go in the box with the car on it." He can sort the socks and the silverware or the toys at school. Later on, get him a daily schedule book and teach him to write in it all of the things he enjoys doing. Post a school calendar and write class activities on it. This device will also help with developing a sense of time, for he can be taught to count the days himself before a family vacation or field trip and quit asking you all the time! After a while, when he's used to it, add homework assignments. Buy, or suggest that his parents buy, subject matter notebooks with pockets for finished assignments so maybe they can be found when it's time to hand them in.

Try not to do more for him than you absolutely must, whether you are teacher or parent, for he will learn from each activity he does, but not from the ones you do for him. Sometimes it seems much easier to do it ourselves, but that does not help them develop skills. Recently, my daughter was redecorating her room, and she and two friends hung the new curtains one evening. The next day I noticed that of the four curtain panels, only one was right side up. I pointed out the difference to her and her response was, "Well, that's what you get for having three L.D.'s hang the curtains!" So we laughed and rehung them together; the important thing is, I think she'll know how to hang curtains next time.

My boys were wrestling in the living room, which they were not supposed to do. They broke the bookcase. I said, "Okay, this happened because you were doing something you were not supposed to do. You figure out how to get it fixed in time for my dinner party on Friday." They did. Years later, they told me how they had to beg and plead with a workman to get it done, but they never broke the bookcase again.

I am aghast at the things my college age students at the university do not know how to do, such as peeling a potato or carving a pumpkin. While I can understand a parent's reluctance at having a child use something with which he might hurt himself, when is he ever going to learn unless we take the time to teach him? I mentioned to my husband that I was about ready to write a research article on "pumpkin-carving behavior," so he organized the first annual pumpkin-carving contest, where everyone could win a prize. We can't keep them away from knives forever; how will they learn to prepare food? I only wish they didn't have to learn all of this on my deck.

We must prepare children as best we can for any situation, and then we have to stand back and let them try it on their own. My son still carries the scar from an axe wound on his finger, from attempting to chop wood at scout camp. He missed. Of course it upset me, even more so his father, who was there at the time, especially since Lance wanted to be a doctor. But, he's chopped a great deal of wood since that time and he did survive. I wonder what he would be like today, if I had restricted his development because I was so fearful of physical harm?

Tara was also active in scouts. As a teenager, she wanted to join the Search and Rescue Squad. This scout activity involved learning to rappel over and down and, it was hoped, up the cliffs in Southern Illinois in search of lost hikers or hunters. Parents were invited to see a slide show of the troop's activities prior to our children's enrollment. After the slide show, Tara said, "Mama, wasn't it wonderful?" "Yes," I answered, "and you may never do it again." I was scared silly. I remembered the dreadful experience of her trying to ride her two-wheeled bike. She wanted those training wheels off; nobody else still had them at eight years of age, but her balance was not good and she constantly fell, receiving, in a mother's eye, terrible wounds. I hated it and dreaded every trial. My husband would run along beside her, but he could not catch her every time. For a while I was mad at both of them every time they tried. As a teenager, she became a long-distance biker. I allowed her to join Search and Rescue, which she still does, and my heart is still in my throat every time she goes out, but I learned long ago that I had to free her to become herself. I had to learn that if my children were being properly supervised, the fear was my problem, not theirs and that in order for them to grow I had to free them from my fears. A sense of organization developed from each of these activities. Chopped wood falls down if not stacked properly, and one must have all the equipment one needs to be safe rappeling, but I wish I didn't know that.

We learned to teach them stalling techniques. Many of our L.D. people have word-finding difficulties and cannot come up with an immediate response when they are asked a question. Give them phrases to use until they can organize what they want to say. Examples might be: "Let me think about that a moment," or "That is a good question." People will wait if they think a response is coming.

In the same manner, analyze his behavior. Pick out the most important behavior to change or improve and concentrate on those. Try not to be critical; instead, couch your comments in such terms as: "I have noticed that sometimes you seem uncomfortable in situations where you are meeting someone new. Let's talk about that." An L.D. teacher in West Virginia heard me speak about this. One of her students could not get along with his shop teacher, although he liked the class and was good at woodworking. She sat down with the boy and gave him one instruction for that day: to walk into the class, say "Good morning, Mr. Greer," and go directly to his seat. On the second day, she told him to say, "Good morning, Mr. Greer. Boy, I really like woodworking," and to go to his seat. By the end of the week, the shop teacher stopped by to tell the L.D. teacher that he couldn't get over the remarkable change in that boy, and what a fine student he had become.

Never, never ridicule a child. A sentence that includes "you never" or "you always" is not to be used. Wrong behavior is frightening to parents because of its implications, but unless the child is in really serious trouble, a subject covered in another chapter, it is probable that he did not realize the consequences of his actions. One of my students washed his parents' car with bleach. On television, bleach gets colors and whites really clean, doesn't it? He was nineteen at the time. No parent is a saint, but try to analyze before you scream.

Determine parental goals and those of the L.D. person. If they are the same, the only thing one needs to work out with him are the steps necessary to attain that goal. Too often, though, the goals of parents and child are far apart educationally, socially, and emotionally. Every adolescent begins to develop his own priorities, and he often places his social goals ahead of his educational goals. If his parents do not realize, from their own teenage years, this basic adolescent need or if it is in conflict with their beliefs and goals, the home can become a battleground. In everything from money to religion the adolescent needs to find his way, to question. I remember visiting churches and synagogues other than my own. My parents were very wise and let me try other religions even though they were very active in church. In adulthood, I became active in the church of my childhood. It is very important for parents to realize that of the activities of adolescence, the old adage of this too shall pass is important to remember. I really don't think that Ted's hair will stay pink very long. It's a current campus fad which his father finds incomprehensible. However, there is still the need to direct and explain when one can. One of my students told me how much he respected a friend who was devoting his life to Christ by becoming a rabbi. I think he's a bit confused.

A family I know has a teenage son who does poorly academically. He does poorly in school because it is the only control he has over his own life. His parents made a bad mistake by relating virtually every activity to his grades. He couldn't get his room decorated until he got good grades; his waterbed would stay in the basement until he got good grades; he couldn't drive the family car until he got good grades. When they finally came to me, there was open hostility among the family members. The parents did not approve of their son, and both expressed dislike of him, not his behavior, in his presence. He feels isolated; the parents are frustrated and everyone is angry with everyone else. He wasn't allowed to drive, so he took the keys and went joy riding at four in the morning. At their first appointment with me, the boy ran away, his father ran after him, and the mother cried beside me. It was a very sad situation.

The situation can be corrected, if all will agree to attempt it. Right now, their home should be classified as a disaster area and one would think that they would do anything to correct the current conflict, but I am not sure they will. Parents and child feel the rightness of their own positions and until they are capable of compromise and really want peace, little progress will be made.

Conflict between adolescent and parent is a common occurrence in every home, as children seek to find their own way. They test us, sorting out the values of their acquaintances against those with which they have been raised. It is a time when the lower one's self-esteem, the less one can be different. The school football hero's mother can forget to wash his shirt and he can come to school in some strange outfit and start a new fad. The same incident can be a tragedy of the highest proportion to the L.D. student, because the less comfortable he is with himself, the more he has to be like everyone else. When parents don't approve of a hairstyle or a style of dress, conflict can occur. Still, parents need to understand how great the child's need is to be like others.

Teachers can be of help to parents by discussing current fads and what is going on at school. The teenage years are generally trying for all concerned. My own father laughingly said to me, "I can't imagine raising four teenagers like you!" And I was a good kid! However, I've lived through four teenagers and given the fact that I haven't seen the telephone in years and clouds of steam constantly spread from the bathroom door, I do understand his comment.

We learned to make as few rules as possible and make those absolute. For instance: "I must always know where you are, and I must always know whom you're with." Set a curfew that is in keeping with the curfew of other students he knows. Put a list of rules in a prominent spot and make sure that everybody abides by them, including the parents. "Do as I say, not as I do," does not work with L.D. people. They will do as you do.

Include children in planning for family and school activities. The very best vacation we ever took was one that the children planned. We had three weeks of vacation, so I told them that each of them could pick three places to see, and it could be anywhere on the east coast. We lived in North Carolina at the time, and could use it as a home base. One child wanted to visit several government sites and the F.B.I. building in Washington, D.C. One was interested in the Salem witch trials and *The House of the Seven Gables*. One was entranced with the musical *1776* and wanted to see places associated with Abigail and John Adams and Thomas Jefferson. Another wanted to visit Civil War battle sites.

They had to plan the trip, picking routes to use, distances between sites so we would know where to spend the night, budgets for gas and motels. They had to keep us on the right road, for we would drive only where they told us to go. We traveled to Maine and Florida and places in between, stopping off at home to wash our clothes. We had a wonderful time. There were no arguments because each child had had a part in planning, and this was his trip. They not only learned map reading, adding, and budgeting but from each other's interests as well. I learned from that trip that I should include them more in family planning. They had good ideas!

Parents of L.D. people need to realize how rigid many of them seem to be, seeing things as black or white and absolutely never any gray. This rigidity surfaces in everything from political issues to his girl friend, to his fury over some real or imagined slight. It is hard to keep calm while trying to convince a person to look at the issue from a slightly different perspective. Recently, my husband and I were trying to direct our daughter's choice of college courses since she was not certain which major to pursue. She really did not want to discuss it. We stayed calm and quietly explained why she needed to consider other factors. After a long time, she finally listened and ended the conversation by saying, "All right, I'll look into it. Boy, parents sure can confuse you!" In the end, she took the courses we had suggested, but had we gotten angry or pushed too hard, she would have become entrenched in her position and unmovable. We are the mature adults. Our L.D. people may not be at that level yet. We need to quietly lead and direct, and to develop the patience of Job.

We learned to share our emotions, to tell them how we were feeling: "I am cross today; I am hurting today; I am confused. This is what happened, what do you think I should do?" Then listen and give feedback. "That's an idea, but I'm afraid if I do that this might occur." This sharing will also enable L.D. people to begin to make a visual association between how a person looks and the words he is saying. Remember, L.D. people do not read faces well, and the more they are included in such discussions, the more they will understand and the more they will be willing to share.

A major area of concern for many parents of L.D. people is the apparent lack of judgment exhibited by their children. They manage to get into so much trouble by not anticipating the outcomes of their actions or the end results of their actions. Parents sometimes wonder how they could possibly do such a thing; the other children would never dream of doing that, and so it goes. Believe me, at some time or other, I have said all of the above; when the black deck became splattered with white paint, when the cat received a detergent bath. Of more concern were those instances when a child did what others told him to do without a second thought. Paul set the school on fire because some boys told him to. It may have seemed like a great idea to Paul; he was not particularly fond of school, but you can imagine his parents' reaction when the police arrived at their door.

Judgment of what is all right to say and do can be taught. The best method for parents and teachers to use is to talk about it with the child rather than to lecture him. This means explaining situations, asking him what he thinks will happen, and showing him how it is correct or incorrect. The evening meal is a good opportunity for parents, providing such discussions are kept free of criticism. Car rides or family outings provide other opportunities for interactions. Enough things happen to our families and friends for us to begin to develop such skills by example in a nonthreatening way. For instance, without asking her father, Jill let a friend borrow his car. What do you think he should do? Teresa talked Tara into driving her someplace, so Tara was late getting home and was grounded. What should Tara do or have done so this would not happen to her again? These same kinds of discussions can take place in the classroom.

Never be afraid to say, "I made a mistake," "I really blew it this time." If parents and teachers can't say it, how are children to learn that it's okay to fail sometimes, that even though a person makes mistakes he can still be a worthwhile, lovable individual?

We learned to involve the other children in the family discussions, but never to allow criticism of one another. We accepted only positive statements and comments, thus teaching our children that home is a place where they can express opinions, receive feedback, and still feel good about themselves. All brothers and sisters fight sometimes, but name calling or hitting are never allowed. Respect for one another, and one another's opinions, will benefit the L.D. person enormously, as well as the other children. The same thing should be true in every L.D. classroom.

Students with learning disabilities who come from large families have fewer socialization problems than those who come from small families. They have learned to interact. Older brothers and sisters can help a great deal if they are included. My older children helped the younger ones learn to drive, to cook, to dance.

We learned to identify a skill we felt our child needed. First we analyzed what aspects of their problems bothered us and why, and then identified the skill we thought was missing. Other parents can do the same thing. Perhaps the child learning to drive cannot consistently remember left from right. Tape a symbol on either side of the dashboard like this: ←L R→. I had one of my students do this. He left off the arrows and told anyone who asked that it was the initials of his girl friend back home!

We taught them to read maps, first around town and later on trips we took. Most chambers of commerce provide city maps free of charge. By enhancing the directional markings on the map, pointing out the direction in which you are traveling, and the position of the sun, L.D. people can learn these driving skills. Point out familiar landmarks and their locations. Remember that many L.D. people do not notice such things as where the bank or grocery store are located. One of my graduate students who has learning disabilities told me that she had traveled the same road for eleven years going to work, but she could never tell where she was on the road and so could not judge how far she still had to travel. Driver Education teachers should be aware of these things.

If a child has a date or a job interview, drive the route with him ahead of time so he will arrive on time and in an unagitated state. I once called a friend who has L.D. and told her I was coming to town. I asked her if she would like to meet me and drive to a school whose administrators said they were "curing" L.D. She said she would love to. She met me at the airport and we talked as we drove to the school, a restaurant, and to her home through city streets and on super highways. She had a list of directions and I thought nothing of the trip we had taken.

Several months later she sent me a tape, telling me how grateful she was that I had had such faith in her to ask her to make that trip. She had gained such self-confidence from the excursion that she later drove to her aunt's house in another state, something she previously would never have dreamed of doing. Such a little thing, and I had not consciously planned any of it. I simply expected her to be able to do it and indeed she could. She needed only the impetus. Provide the impetus for children and expect that they will be successful. Don't assume that they are staying home because they want to; they may not know how to get where they want to be.

We learned to teach them to watch for road signs and speed limit signs. Remember that if a person's reading is labored, he will have trouble reading road signs rapidly. It will be helpful to get a driving manual to use in teaching the colors of signs to which he must pay attention. Then he will learn that he must pay attention to signs that are red, orange, yellow, or white because they are safety-related, and can ignore the ones that are brown or green, which are informational. One father said, "Well that sounds good, but how do I get him to pay attention? Too often he just walks away, even when I'm trying to teach him something he really needs to learn. It's very frustrating." Of course it is, but we must remember that the medical description of L.D. is attentional deficit disorder; that means his attention span will be short. Most of us talk too much. Show him the colors in the driving manual, on several occasions if necessary. He will catch on eventually and will also probably study it on his own if no one is watching.

When the family goes out, let him drive. This gives a parent the opportunity to point out the good and bad elements of his driving and to offer suggestions.

We learned to teach them about car registration and insurance policies, and what to do in case of an accident; to teach them the basic mechanics of the car and how to change a flat. Do not assume that he knows.

Virtually every aspect of his life should be analyzed and structured this way, whether it be grocery shopping and fixing a meal or determining which is the better buy on a stereo. Take him with you shopping and explain why you are choosing one item over another. Confidence builds confidence and each new ability moves him closer to the mainstream of life. My friend learned to drive to her aunt's; who knows where she will go this year, and isn't it wonderful?

6

EVERYONE ALWAYS SEEMS TO BE BUSY
RELATIONSHIPS—DEVELOPING AND KEEPING THEM

Positive relationships with others is a major goal for most of us. We all need to feel acceptance from our peer group, from people we meet socially, and from those with whom we must live and work.

ADOLESCENCE

At his Individual Educational Program (I.E.P.) meeting with me this year, Dan wanted to add "to get a girl" to his long-range goals. Although we laughed, we both knew that he was interested in the topic. In other words, he's normal.

Walk through any high school corridor and you will see the beginnings of male-female relationships. Peer relationships are the most important agenda item for any teenager. Each has discovered the opposite sex, although for the learning disabled in particular, what to do with it may pose a question. Handicap, or lack of one, has absolutely nothing to do with this basic human need, except in terms of how successful one may be in filling it.

By the time learning disabled people are adolescents, many no longer feel good about themselves as people. I think all teenagers go through phases of self-doubt. I remember hating my nose for a while and telling my mother I had Kermit the Frog eyes. She quietly said, "Well, dear, it all seems to come together well." With the learning disabled, once again we are talking about a matter of degree, for their self-doubt is deeper and more pervasive than that of the average teenager. In truth, academic failures and continual wounding of the ego are realities, and so their feelings of self-doubt, of being rejected by others, are not abnormal but may be based in reality. Because they are unsure of others' responses to them or what those responses may mean, peer relationships that should have been founded during preadolescent years are often not present. The L.D. person wasn't liked then; he isn't liked now. Shrunken into himself, he wishes he could walk down the hall unseen and unnoticed.

When one is ashamed of what one is, the tendency is to withdraw into oneself; the eyes look down, the shoulders hunch forward, in such obvious contrast to the football hero who strides along, head held high, greeting people as he passes. The entire demeanor of the person with L.D. may say to all who notice, "I am worthless; pardon me for taking space in your world."

In stark contrast is the learning disabled person who lacks impulse control. Striking out orally or physically at teachers or fellow students, he tends to frighten those around him and spends a lot of time in the principal's office. Those who are not like him do not understand him and seek to avoid him. For both types, it is a lonely world. Neither type knows how to change the situation.

Audition has been called the social sense, for in communicating with others, we talk. In high school, college, or the work place, peer relationships usually begin with light conversation. One comments on the game, the work load, the weather, and receives light comments in turn from the one addressed, unless one has a learning disability. Consider the components of successful conversation. One person approaches another (making certain not to invade his life-space), gains eye contact, and makes a simple statement. If he invades the life-space of another, that person's discomfort level is instantly raised; if he holds his head down and mumbles something, the person addressed will either try to gain eye contact or will reject the comment, and him, and walk away. If he has difficulty talking, he will not usually initiate conversation anyway. What is he to talk about? Certainly not the latest book, or even last night's football game. He probably did not go. It's no fun to be by yourself when everyone else is in a group, or so it seems. If he perseverates in talking, soon the other person will attempt an escape. Every one of these nonacademic disabilities can disrupt the most limited social interaction. For our friends, each of us tends to seek out people like ourselves. Because the L.D. person is seen as different, he is usually not sought as a friend unless he is particularly good at some sport. Then it seems to be much less important whether or not he can read, or spell, or talk.

As a result, we see many adolescents who are very depressed. Feeling helpless to change their situation and hopeless about the future, there are few options as far as the L.D. adolescent is concerned. Attempted suicides are high in this group, and those who do not actually attempt suicide often contemplate it. Some succeed, to the loss of all of society.

Others retreat into a fantasy world, building a life in their minds that does not exist in reality. Popular rock and roll stars or television personalities are the favorite choices for fantasy relationships. The walls in his room become covered with pictures and posters and letters from the fan club. Denied normal relations with a peer group, a fantasy love relationship develops which helps to fill, however inadequately, a basic human need. Some count as their friends the postal worker, bus driver, or the man at the delicatessen, substituting these transient, short interactions for the long-term relationship with one person that most people seek.

Quite often, in the beginning of the Achieve Program, we had a problem with our students falling in love with their tutors, many of whom were young girls only four or five years older. A close association with someone you saw often, who knew you were L.D., and who still accepted you, was a heady experience for many of our boys, and one they had not experienced before. They fell madly in love with their tutors, who were only trying to help and who usually did not share the feeling. We had to take steps to stop it, for it got in the way of education, but it taught me about their very real hunger for relationships.

Loneliness is no fun. We all want and need to be hugged and loved. A dear friend, herself an L.D. adult, knew I was writing this book and wanted me to understand some of her feelings. "This is the first time I've been able to verbalize my need for affection. I was always just sliding up to someone, trying to get a hug anytime I could get one. I can remember thinking that the only time I could get a hug was if I looked sad, so I looked sad. Every time you hugged me, I loved it, but inside I was so afraid I would revert to the child feelings. You see, when someone would hug me, I would feel like a child. This is the place I am safe, loving me, loving the child inside of me. I remember the warmth and comfort I would feel.

"When I was hugged as a child, I would cling and not want to let go. I'm now afraid of losing people. I have lost so many people by clinging too much, that now I am afraid to show emotion. The emotions are in me so deep that now I'm afraid to allow myself to feel."

Relationships which are formed, and this can be at any age, are often suffocating to the non-learning disabled partner. We have had many problems with this at the university level, because of our students' difficulties in dealing with relationships. Once a relationship is formed, it becomes all-encompassing. Jake was so eager to join the Achieve Program that he "would walk to get here!" from Florida. But, once here, he could not bear to be away from his girl friend. His weekends became longer and longer, and finally he simply failed to return. Another's girl friend broke up with him and he could not deal with it. He developed heavy drug use and eventually left school.

The breakup of any type of relationship can be traumatic and threatening, but, again, it often happens because the L.D. person smothers the other in a relationship, and demands more than anyone else is really able to give. Clinging to spouse, children, friend, or therapist, the L.D. person sees any attempt to put some distance between such people and himself as a danger, and it may produce genuine anguish and fear on his part. It can be very threatening to lose an important part of one's support system. Often we even see rage when we assign a new tutor to a student, for the student may feel that he has been abandoned, no matter how competent the new tutor may be, or for what reason the change was made.

A part of this stems from the fact that many young people with L.D. have been rejected in the past. When they find someone who knows about their disability, and likes them and tries to help them anyway, there is a tremendous fear that this support system might be lost, and they will be plunged back into that morass of loneliness so familiar in the past. In order to prevent that possibility from happening, they tend to do the thing which is most likely to destroy a relationship—hold on too tightly. As sand filters through the fingers when held too tightly in the hands, so the relationship clutched too tightly slips away.

It is hard to be needed that much, especially by someone who looks like an adult. Another therapist and I were having coffee after a long day and he said that when he went home at night, he felt as though he needed to pull off leeches that all day had been trying to devour him. He loved working with his clients and they adored him, but each of us has only so much he can give, and L.D. people can be excessively demanding. Sometimes it seems that we who understand them are making up for all the people who did not understand or accept them in the past. Some therapists burn out, and feel they must stop working with a client, a situation that often causes a downward spiral for the L.D. person who sees it as the ultimate abandonment. I have seen severe depression and genuine grief of long duration even when the new therapist is just as loving, just as helpful. Dependency is the major factor. The adolescent or adult person with learning disabilities may feel that he is so inadequate, so incomplete, that his very identity is dependent on someone else. When that support is withdrawn, for whatever reason, to him it may feel as a loss of self as well.

We all remember young love, that exhilarating agony and ecstasy when we can think of nothing but the loved one. It may only last a week or two with each successive love object, yet most of us begin to experience those feelings at fourteen or so, which gives us all those high school years when others are as awkward as we are to learn how to act and what to say. We develop a level of sophistication through learning acceptable behavior. L.D. people are usually much older before they move into these stages of growth and it is by no means uncommon for our twenty-year-old college students to be in the first throes of puppy love. This is a problem for many of them, for the people they want to be with are close to their own ages and have gone through those stages years ago. The levels of sophistication in getting and maintaining relationships between the L.D. person and the non-L.D. person may be far removed from each other.

YOUNG ADULTHOOD

When I was program chairman of the 1982 International Association for Children and Adults with Learning Disabilities convention, I was discussing with the committee some topics which I felt needed to be highlighted in the program. I mentioned marital problems in particular, to which a committee member, and L.D. adult, replied, "Marriage problems! Heck, Barb, tell us how to get close to others in the first place!"

Good point. All of those needs, mentioned in the section on adolescence, are still present in the young adult, in addition to the need for further education or employment. Each area can pose problems for the individual without L.D. Consider what it may be like for the person with learning disabilities.

It is the rare person with L.D. who is in the social whirl. Unless by accident of birth, by an unusual athletic ability, or by particularly successful achievement in a specific area, where one finds oneself accepted, the individual with learning disabilities finds the prospect for developing relationships grim. Where do we meet people? Generally we meet new people on the job, in our college classes, or at other activities we might pursue such as a club, church, or synagogue. First of all, the L.D. young adult, unsure of himself and fearful, probably doesn't belong to any clubs. He is uncomfortable with himself and with others. More importantly, he will have problems responding to others in most situations.

Most of us begin relationships by looking a little too long at someone, and smiling when we catch his eye. Yet, many L.D. adults tell how very difficult it is for them to derive meaning from those subtle social cues. Indeed, they don't know how to make those little social advances themselves. They report that they are often unsure if their faces and body language are really sending the message they want to convey. They may find themselves being approached when they don't want to be and not approached when they really want attention. It is a confusing world.

Over breakfast, Dale Brown, herself an L.D. adult, said, "You know, the major problem of being socially disabled is that you don't know you are!" Dale has written extensively of her own difficulties in forming associations with others and the steps she took to overcome those difficulties. Her difficulties were not unique. Modulation of voice; either lack of eye contact or, by contrast, staring; difficulties with small talk or touching—all contribute to the L.D. person's difficulty in developing relationships of whatever kind.

Relationships begin and develop through language. When we're interested in someone, we try to appear bright and charming. When we're in love, there is so much we want to share. Words of endearment, murmurs of contentment, loving thoughts, all are a part of the relationship. When one has difficulty expressing these things, one is handicapped right from the beginning and a relationship that might have been special may never really get started.

Difficulties in developing relationships are not restricted to the opposite sex only, for those things that set a person apart can affect all relationships. Fitting in with a group requires that one conducts oneself as do others within that group. The person who behaves inappropriately, asks impertinent questions, or laughs too loudly is quickly rejected by the group and is also rejected by individuals.

Social consciousness is really an understanding of how one behaves in society. We have to know how to act around others and what responses are appropriate for a situation. A young man was sitting at a cafeteria table working with his tutor. At a nearby table, a woman was talking and laughing rather loudly. The student could not concentrate on his work and wanted to go over and, as he said, "punch her out." Such reactions are common with the L.D. person, whose response to situations that others might laugh off or ignore may be completely out of line. The young man's tutor told him they would just move to another table, a socially accepted response, but without her help, he would not have understood that moving was also an option.

These kinds of behaviors are part of what has been called a repertoire of behaviors, meaning that an individual understands that in any situation there are several ways one can respond. The socially disabled person does not have this repertoire, so the response of desiring to punch someone, which might be appropriate if a man's wife is insulted, is applied to all situations.

Max wanted to meet lovely Sandra, a woman he had seen several times, and finally talked Joe into introducing him. "Sandra, I'd like you to meet Max. Max is an engineer. Max, this is Sandra. She's an art student." Max reached over and tweaked her nose. Neither Max nor Joe has seen her since.

People tweak children on the nose in an affectionate way. Max could not understand why that had been offensive to Sandra. He later said, "I don't know why I can't get a date. Everyone always seems to be busy." A perfect time to begin to teach social skills to the L.D. person is when such a comment is made. One might say, "Tell me how you asked her out; what did you say?" Role play if you need to.

Inability to take the blame for what one has done is another common problem. Allen was two hours late for his appointment. It was not his fault, he said. The place where he was staying hadn't set an alarm for him. Of course he hadn't asked them to set an alarm, but, he said, "they should have known." Another said his boss was unreasonable, so he had fixed the boss; he didn't show up for work and he didn't call. He was fired, of course, and believed in the righteousness of his anger over such cruel treatment.

Whether the person with L.D. is looking for a date or a job, the steps should be outlined in advance. Talking through the dialogue, giving the L.D. person an opportunity to role play the situation, is a good starting point. Picking a restaurant, going there ahead of time and looking at a menu will make him more comfortable when he takes his date there.

Getting a date in the first place may be scary. How to ask her out is one thing, but what do I do if she says yes? What can I talk about? Usually it's best to go places where one doesn't have to talk much, such as to a movie or to a rock concert. School sporting events are usually all right because one's comments can be short and to the point, the terrific play someone made or the obvious eye problem of the referee.

There is also another side of the coin—the L.D. person who for some reason seems to draw others to him whether or not he is capable of conversation. One such young man developed a whole life style around very short-term relationships—one night at a time, showing no judgment whatsoever. When I took this job, I never knew I'd also have to teach sex education!

Strong, silent Bill, who talked very little, had a succession of girls following him around, but he, unlike most, handled it very well. He staged a fake dinner party, invited the girls, and brought his cousin, whom he introduced as his fiancée. Assuming then that he already had a permanent girl friend, the others left him alone. However, the important fact remains that neither Max nor Bill is able to form long-term relationships at this point in their lives.

Getting a job requires many of the same social skills as getting a date. One of my former students, a marketing major, wanted to work for a large pharmaceutical company in her home state. She applied for the job in an adjoining state, went in for a personal interview, took notes on the questions which were asked, and took the required test. She was not hired. She applied in the next state, went through the whole process again, and was offered a low ranking job, which she did not accept. She then applied in her home state, confident and self-assured because she knew what was to come. She was hired in the job she wanted and has been with the company for five years now, continuing to progress in her field. The ability had always been there, but the process needed to be taught.

That student felt comfortable and won her job because she had practiced applying for it. Our L.D. people do not choose to be lonely or out of work, but they don't know how to change the situation. We, as their parents, therapists, teachers, friends, and mentors, must teach them.

MARRIED LIFE

If one has managed to get through all of these difficulties and gets married, problems may still exist, for a person with learning disabilities may pose special problems for a spouse. Everyone who has ever been married is aware that big arguments over disciplining the children, finances, and in-laws are, in most cases, relatively rare. It is the everyday issues that cause most of the unpleasant times. It must also be stated that many L.D. adults are unaware of their specific disabilities because there were no L.D. programs when they were growing up. They know they do not function as others do, but don't know why.

I was speaking before a group of teachers in a three-day inservice workshop. They were enthusiastic and responsive. By the first afternoon, I noticed that a lovely young woman who had been in the first row was now at the back, in a corner. On the second day, she seemed to respond less often and kept her head down. On the third day she sat huddled on the floor and remained there all day.

Everyone left except for the two of us. I slowly packed up my materials and waited. She began to cry softly, her face buried in her knees. As I knelt beside her, she threw her arms around me and sobbed uncontrollably. "My husband says I'm so stupid. My whole family has always said so. I drop things; I lose things; I can't find my way around town. Last night I nearly burned down the kitchen because, you know, I have one of those counter top stoves with buttons down one side; I can never remember which one goes to which burner. My husband yells at me. I teach first grade because I can spell those words, but I still mix up left and right and sometimes I have to ask the children."

"What has caused you so much grief has a name, learning disabilities," I said. "It is not your fault; you are not stupid. Think about all that I have taught you in the last three days. This all comes as a shock to you, but it should be a good shock. Now you know you're not stupid, no matter what anyone has said." We talked for a long time, and then a friend, to whom she had obviously confessed her fears, came in and hugged her. They left together; she had some thinking to do, and some adjusting.

It certainly was easier for female L.D.'s in the past than it is today. Women who were unsuccessful academically could marry young and stay home and raise their babies. Even if they were poorly organized, things eventually got done or they were simply thought of as poor housekeepers. The degree of stress caused by L.D. really depended more on what one's husband required and the degree of organizational abilities one possessed or lacked. Kim got out the frozen meat when her husband walked in the door, every single day, so they normally ate dinner at eleven or twelve at night. He couldn't cope with her lack of organizational ability and eventually divorced her. There are always solutions if one seeks them. An obvious solution would have been for him to remove the meat each morning, but he was not that sort of man. It was her job, and because neither of them understood, they didn't know how to solve their differences. It isn't always easy to live with a person with L.D., for no matter what his disability is, the nonhandicapped spouse must take over all responsibilities in that area. Ideally, the nonhandicapped spouse should be slowly teaching the skill to the degree possible, but that doesn't mean that he or she won't occasionally get irritated about it. A wife finds herself having to say, "Dear, the movie starts in fifteen minutes," to the husband who knows when the movie starts, but who has made no move to get off the couch. She expects to tell their kids to get ready; but she resents having to keep reminding her husband.

To make matters worse, women's roles have changed significantly in recent years. Women used to be judged on how well they married, and their status came from their husbands' occupations. Now, as more than 40 percent of married women also work outside the home and compete in the marketplace, the problem has become much more complex. Very few of those women come home to a dinner prepared and a home cleaned by a maid. Organizational skills are essential to get it all done. Obviously, some people detest house cleaning, have husbands who don't care whether it's clean or not, and as a result, clean very little. I know a couple of fellow teachers who apologize for their homes all the time but don't do anything about them. That is very different from the woman with learning disabilities who wants to keep a clean house and have dinner ready on time, and expresses wonder about how anyone ever accomplishes it. Molly used to tell me how she tried to clean up the living room. She would pick up something, carry it to the room in which it belonged, put it down, having spotted something there which was in the wrong place. The result was that no room ever got cleaned although she worked hard to accomplish it. Only after trying Ritalin, a drug that helps some L.D. people organize their lives better, did it occur to her that one should remove all the dishes from the table and carry them to the kitchen, and then start to wash them.

At a learning disabilities' conference, a somewhat disheveled young woman tried to keep her little baby contented and her two-year-old quiet. As the meeting progressed, the baby started to cry and the mother, trailed by the two-year-old, stepped over people to get to the door. When the baby quieted, they would come back in. This happened so many times that the meeting was disrupted and people became somewhat irritated. During the question-and-answer period it became obvious from the desperate nature of her shouted questions that she was an L.D. adult who was experiencing overwhelming problems in dealing with her personal life with two small children. Even though her attempts to find help were seen as inappropriate and irritating to others, at least she realized that she needed help and had come to the only place she knew to try to find it. The L.D. experts who were speaking took her aside and tried to help her. It is often easier for L.D. specialists to help simply because they understand the disability while the marital partners may not.

It can be very hard for the marital partners to remember that much of the irritating behavior is not willful. It is not the spilling of the milk that is so frustrating, it is the inevitability of having the milk spilled. Spouses can almost predict what is going to cause trouble, and because they can, they may become irritable in anticipation of something that may not even happen. The scenario starts like this. It's Saturday, a gorgeous day, and he wants to plant the garden, something he enjoys. He plants, waiting, knowing he will not be able to finish—that just when he's in the middle of something his wife will need his help. In a way, it makes the spouse feel good to be needed; the gratefulness of the mate is real, so the spouse feels appreciated. It can be very ego satisfying to be around someone who needs you all the time, especially during the early courtship days. But, such needy people can be very wearing at the end of a busy day after some of the starshine has dimmed. The cycle develops kinks in it when the husband wants to do something for himself and the needs of his wife continually interrupt. Yet, if a woman has a supportive, loving husband who will assume those duties she can't manage and who will help her learn the skills she must learn, she will be able to function satisfactorily. Too often, though, it does not happen that way, for just as it is difficult for parents to demand that their children try to do things that are difficult for them, so it is hard for the spouse to demand that the mate try to accomplish the difficult task. A woman may have an easier time with L.D. than a man, for society sometimes allows her to be helpless.

However, there is a danger in such helplessness. For a variety of reasons, most often in the name of love, people do more than they should for the learning disabled person who is cherished. A dear friend, Nonnie Star, lost her husband unexpectedly. Not only did she have to deal with his death but with the things Carl had always done for her. She had a home on the shore, but she didn't know how to get there. Checking accounts, insurance policies, car registrations—all of those kinds of things with which we all must deal in society, were, to her, unknowns. In a sense, by doing everything for her, he, through love, had handicapped her further, Nonnie said.

A man's role is considered differently in industrial countries. Whereas a woman may or may not have to work outside the home, men are more often socialized to expect to hold a job and to assume the family's major financial responsibility. Most learning disabled men do just that. Many hold jobs of significant importance in their companies. Others, who perhaps had fewer choices, work at occupations well beneath their abilities and are thereby frustrated. They may be very difficult to live with and may take out some of their frustration on their families. These men may also be disorganized. One of the things a wife I know has found most troubling to deal with is the quantity of things her husband collects. It seems she can never keep the house clean for more than five minutes at a time. Papers, articles—all kinds of things repose in various boxes and envelopes with no organization. There is no one box for cards and letters, no one box for maps, and so forth, and, like most wives, her attempts to organize are not uniformly appreciated.

Some L.D. husbands are forced to keep up appearances at work—to hide their disabilities because of the impact they are likely to have on co-workers and supervisors. To sustain such pretenses can be tiring, and so when the L.D. person gets home, he just wants to relax and not be forced into any more decision making or responsibilities. For his wife, who may also have an outside job, this situation can seem very unfair. In addition, many wives complain that they tend to lead somewhat isolated lives, for while they need other friends, their husbands don't. It takes energy to have L.D. and survive in a non-L.D. world, and so the wife may need to find other outlets for her social needs.

Many other responsibilities fall on the wives of learning disabled men as well. Lily has to handle the finances because Tyrell forgets to pay the bills on time. Obviously, those with math disabilities would have difficulty in this area too. Every bill, every circular, every letter, may have to be read and dealt with by the wife. School reports, homework, holiday cards—virtually every aspect of their lives and those of their children may have to be taken care of by the nonhandicapped spouse. Sometimes this condition is devastating to a relationship.

A young wife I know explains that if she is working late and asks her husband to start dinner, he is very willing to try, but that he may call her three or four times while trying to cook up a box of macaroni and cheese. This kind of thing can cause friction because personal calls are discouraged at work and one does get tired of being asked the same questions repeatedly. But she loves him very much and is most supportive of his efforts to improve; and although she must bear an added burden, their marriage should endure.

Sadly, for many, their marriages are at risk, and the divorce rate for unremediated learning disabled people seems inordinately high. There are numerous possible reasons for this high rate. Language is our major form of communication; if one is disabled in this area, one can misunderstand what is said and take offense. My husband and I used to have real problems with this as I was told time and again that I had said something I knew I hadn't said. With both of us certain of the correctness of our positions, there was no room for anything except confrontation. We learned that when he heard something which seemed offensive, he should ask me again; I learned to ask what he thought he had heard.

All spouses like to hear nice things; they like to be told they are loved and appreciated. They like to be complimented. Those with expressive language problems don't do that well, even though they may feel it emotionally. If a wife buys her husband a new jacket as a surprise and expects to hear, "What a thoughtful thing to do, honey; let's see how it fits," but, instead, he looks at it, holds it up, and says only, "Looks too small," she may not care whether he has a jacket or not. What she had considered a thoughtful, loving thing to do resulted in her feeling unappreciated.

Thus if one's major means of communication is limited, misperceptions, misunderstandings, reinforcement, even expressions of love can be problem areas. All of the potential difficulties discussed in previous chapters in some ways become more acute in the intimacy of marriage. The tactilely defensive individual who could not bear to wear the new blue jeans may still have trouble with light touching. Some L.D. adults tell me they feel the fight-or-flight response when touched—they literally feel like hitting whoever touched them or running away. Some speak of feeling a burning sensation when touched, while most respond normally when the touch is firm. One can understand how such responses can affect a relationship. When one understands the various aspects of a disability, one can take steps to avoid a problem before it occurs. If one does not understand, it is very easy for one's spouse to get most irritated or even to terminate the marriage.

Nick did leave, and he was the marital partner with learning disabilities. Nick is very bright, with a Ph.D. in psychology, but he is very rigid, one of the L.D. adults who tends to see things in all white or all black. Language disabilities made him sometimes misperceive what was said to him, and he took every slight, of whatever kind, and as he said, "swallowed them," keeping them bottled up inside himself where no one could deal with them, neither his wife, who adored him, nor himself. He says now that he doesn't understand why he and his wife didn't get marital counseling; he certainly knew about it. But I know them both and I do not think he would have been willing at the time.

Things are generally getting better now. Earlier identification, if combined with understanding and appropriate remediation and support systems, can lead to better comprehension of the whole issue of learning disabilities. Support groups for L.D. adults offer opportunities for interaction, trips, and new experiences as long as it is the adult part, not the L.D. part, that is emphasized. Employers and timed tests, necessary for employment in many fields, remain problems. Even though untimed testing is now required by federal law to be allowed for all persons with handicaps, many people with L.D. are afraid to ask for this service, thinking that they may be eliminating themselves from the hiring process by doing so.

Helping L.D. persons, their families, and friends to understand the disability is important to all their futures.

I USED TO DREAM THAT I WOULD WAKE UP NORMAL
IMPLICATIONS FOR THE PROFESSIONAL

"I used to dream that I would wake up normal. One day I would just pick up a book and read it like anyone else," Pat said. Pat has dyslexia, a severe disability in reading. Pretty and articulate, she was enrolled in a college program where she was learning to work with handicapped children. As Pat said, "I have a need in me to reach out to others to help them."

Helping others is a common goal among many L.D. people for a variety of reasons. Some want to teach, feeling that understanding learning disabilities as they do they will be better teachers than those who had taught them. Some want to be psychologists; virtually all of them have been tested repeatedly and often misdiagnosed as Pat was. School personnel had said she was retarded, and there she stayed throughout high school. Normally, the Achieve Program does not test retarded people because we know we do not have an adequate program for them, but something about Pat made us choose to look further. She was not retarded, never had been. She's a junior in college now, and doing very well. L.D. people want to do it better. Even when the goal is to be a surgeon or film maker, the desire is often to discover a cure or to make a documentary about learning disabilities.

Such students are responding to the basic human needs of wanting some answers to their problems and hoping to help others avoid the pain which they have felt.

The pain is very real. "I didn't know how to explain to others how I was feeling," Pat said. "I knew I was normal, but there were things I couldn't do, like spell, so I would go home and cry because it was so painful." In the fifth grade, Tim's class took a vote as to who was worse off in the class. It came down to a contest between Tim and "an ugly girl." "She won because there was something she could do; she could paint," Tim said. L.D. people hurt for others, too, not knowing how they are causing the pain, but understanding that somehow, they are at fault. "My mother took me someplace and people in white lab coats took blood samples and put electrodes on my head. They gave me some tests. They called my mother into a room and whatever they told her, she came out crying."

I do not know a single family where there is a person with learning disabilities that has not experienced such pain, for when you have a hurt child, you have a hurt family, too. The variables that determine the depth of those experiences are the degree of understanding that both professionals and parents have about the disability itself, the degree of stability and loving relationships in the family, and the amount of support parent and child receive from significant persons and outside agencies, including the schools.

Another important variable is the value system of the family. Professionally successful parents are more likely to demand academic success than may the family of a manual laborer where college, or even high school, is not seen as a necessary goal. Certain ethnic groups tend to place a higher value on school success than do others. All of these factors, then, impact on the developing adult and his perception of himself, and the primary place where this pain begins is school.

The little boy came home crying again, because another day had gone by and he hadn't received a sticker for good work. His mother went in to talk to the teacher. "Couldn't you find something to give him a sticker for?" she asked. "Frankly, Mrs. Jones, I can't think of anything he does well," the teacher answered. A few days later the little boy came home and said, "Mom, I got a bunny sticker! Well, almost a whole sticker, I got a half sticker. Mom, why would she think I would want a bunny with only one ear?" Teachers who behave as this one did have no right to be surprised when parents actively detest them.

Fortunately, for our mental health, most teachers are more understanding, and those who are not often suffer more from ignorance than from cruelty. A nun said, "I know nothing of learning disabilities and when a student, during a discussion, told me he had dyslexia, I went right in and washed my hands." These are the kinds of problems we, as teachers and other professionals, need to address. Education, as always, is the key.

The nature of the learning disability usually determines how early a student is identified as having a problem in school. If he is severely disabled with problems in writing (dysgraphia), reading (dyslexia), and math (dyscalculia), he is more likely to be identified at an early age now that more and more people know about learning disabilities. He will then be referred for testing, usually with the school psychologist, who may know absolutely nothing about L.D. Special children are usually discussed only minimally in most college school psychology programs, and when they are discussed the tendency is to teach the students about emotional disturbance and mentally retarded students' IQ profiles. Learning disabilities are often difficult to pinpoint and require involved testing procedures to interpret the type of disability. I remember my case load as a school psychologist and the limited amount of time I could spend with each child, and I had been previously trained in L.D. Typing far into the night in order to keep up with the case load and still do an adequate job for each child caused some distress in our home, since my family wanted my time, too. Even so, psychologists should take the time to explain to their subjects just what it is they are doing. Currently, a child or adolescent is pulled out of his class with little or no advance warning and little, if any, explanation. He is asked to do extremely difficult things, and he may not stop until he fails. He gets no feedback and no one ever tells him what it was all about. Only recently, I discussed her test results with a dear friend now in her thirties. The test results were twenty years old. I took a look at the IQ test results and nearly cried, for the results showed that despite the typical patterns of strengths and weaknesses one sees in a normal L.D. individual, her IQ was well within the normal range. "Joan," I said, "who told you that you were retarded?" But she no longer remembered. Everyone had accepted that diagnosis so long ago. It is so wrong for her and her family to have believed that fallacy all this time. All the unnecessary pain, the inappropriate treatment, the feelings she had about her inadequacies should have been addressed many years ago.

A concerned psychologist should take a few mom~ the testing, explaining that everyone has s+ nesses—

so well.

test res

himself. In Dennis' case

ried away with him th

shilling on the tes

word. How did y~

watch a lot of T   ~e

learning disabled, ~   ~iffi-

cult to say something su   ~. Do

you know what that means~   up one

hundred kids just your age, only ~   ~ well as

you did! You are one smart boy!"

The wise psychologist will also listen fo~   ~an just the correct answer. Psychologists tend to be quite goo~ at identifying responses that may indicate behavior problems but less knowledgeable in determining why an answer was given. We must learn to stop and ask. I once said, "What is a diamond?" The little L.D. boy said, "Ten cents." "What did I ask you?" I said. "What is a dime," he answered. His was not a vocabulary problem, but a problem in receptive language.

There is also a tendency, in every field, I believe, to use terminology that others outside the field may find difficult to translate. The end result is that school psychologists' reports often come back to the classroom teacher with very little to offer her in the way of help for the child because of the limited testing, a lack of training of the psychologist, and the use of unfamiliar terms. Teachers complain about this situation all the time, with good reason. What is the good in having a child tested, unless something which will help the child develops from it? Psychologists should not be content with reporting IQ and grade levels. In the first place, the L.D. person is quite likely to do well on one test and very poorly on another, just because one test is timed and the other isn't, or because one is a pencil-and-paper task while the other requires only that the student point to the correct answer. Yet both tests are measuring his math abilities.

When measured by several math tests indicating grade levels, one student's scores were:

KEY MATH (visual and auditory presentation, written and oral responses)	7.6
PIAT (visual and auditory presentation, oral response only)	12.9+
WOODCOCK-JOHNSON (visual and auditory presentation, written and oral responses)	9.7
WRAT (visual presentation only, written responses and timed)	5.6

It should be obvious to the most inexperienced diagnostician that without a task analysis, it is impossible to determine where this student is actually functioning in math.

If the child is determined to be only minimally handicapped, he may stay in the regular classroom. Under existing federal laws, the least restrictive environment (L.R.E.) clause of Public Law 94–142, the Education of All Handicapped Children law, requires that a child spend as much time as possible in the regular education classroom (called mainstreaming) and, based on the severity of his disability, that he be given support in a resource room. A resource room is a class where children receive remediation in whatever areas they need help. How often they go there and how long they stay is unfortunately more often dependent upon the number of identified children in the school than on the needs of the individual student. The child who needs a great deal of help may be placed in a self-contained classroom, which means he will receive all or almost all of his schoolwork in that room. The classroom teacher's perception of the child's needs may have little to

.. ..th what services he actually receives. Of far more importance is the psychologist's report, which may or may not be accu-
rate, and the number of children to be served in that school. Because of these factors, a minimally to moderately handicapped
child may spend half of each day, or only one hour a week receiving services. The variability of the services is profound and
frightening.

So, too, is the perception of these situations by classroom
teachers. It is a sad thing that administrators, superintendents,
and the federal government do not ask classroom teachers what
their opinions are before imposing new rules and regulations
upon them. Public Law 94–142 posed just such a problem. Although the law provided funds to retrain teachers to work with
special children, many districts used the money for training of
questionable value to the teachers when it came to handicapped
children.

Poor training also has other causes. As school enrollments de-
cline across the land, some teachers have gone back to be recer-
tified in special education in order to keep their jobs. Since they
have already completed an education degree, and it can be in just
about anything, the requirements for certification in most states
are two courses. Two courses! Since the teachers have already
done their student teaching, they do not have to student teach
again. So, a teacher who may have been a fine home economics,
shop, or band teacher is allowed to walk into a classroom of learning disabled students, having never taught one before. It is a
shameful situation.

Only a few years ago, not one course in special education was
required for a regular education teacher. As of this writing,
thirty states now require one course, but that is only for students
currently in college, and twenty states don't even have that re-
quirement. It is little wonder that we have the problems we have.
In addition, many teachers are angry about mainstreaming. Over
and over I hear, "If I had wanted to be in special education, I
would have trained in special education. Now I have to write
three sets of lesson plans; one for my regular students, one for

the retarded child, and one for the L.D. child. My work load has tripled, but I sure don't see it in my paycheck!" Although the law was signed in 1975, many are still angry, and one can understand some of that anger. Their points are well taken. The problem is that, as usual, it is the handicapped child who suffers.

— The idea behind mainstreaming was to allow special students to associate with nonhandicapped peers in order to help them to develop the social interactions possible in such settings. L.D. students were to spend those hours in the regular classroom when subjects in which they did well were taught. They were to spend the other hours with the L.D. teacher. While that sounds good on paper, according to these guidelines, the child with dysgraphia should ideally never be in the regular classroom. Although he has no trouble learning the material, there are no elementary or high school classes that require no writing. The solution for him is to stay in class and simply allow him to dictate long assignments and take tests orally, so that he can demonstrate what he has learned instead of being graded on how rapidly he can write; but that adaptation happens in very few schools. Professionals often state that it is wrong to give special considerations to such children, that it is just not fair to the other children. I feel like responding, "Okay, then let's make the child with the broken leg play soccer. It isn't fair for him to get to sit on the bench." Obviously, such statements are made out of ignorance.

Anyone who has ever taught school knows that within the first few days of class the students have figured out that the Redbirds are the good readers and the Bluebirds are the poorer readers. As educators, we go to great lengths to hide such things from our students, even to having a secret numbering system for our textbooks. It's foolish, of course, for the children find out almost immediately. The dyslexic is always the Bluebird, an especially difficult handicap because reading is a part of almost every academic subject area. One has to read story problems in mathematics, chapters and worksheets in social studies, plays and stories in English, experiments in science, and background information in history. The dyslexic individual may read slowly, with poor comprehension, or so poorly that he can't make any sense out of the assignment. He will always be behind.

While he should be receiving appropriate remediation based on his particular learning style, classroom teachers at whatever level can do a great deal to make him more successful in the meantime. One summer I borrowed all the tape recorders that the school district possessed. A local bank donated blank cassette tapes. A service sorority in town was talked into assigning each member a book to record during the summer. As school approached, the taped books were collected and the community college made copies of them at no charge. Sets of the books were distributed to each high school. Each dyslexic was given a set of the taped texts he would need for that term. No longer did his parents have to read to him every night, no longer did he have to depend on others in order to learn the material. He could go to class prepared, knowing the content. He could feel better about himself. Now, we can order textbooks on tape from Talking Books at the Library of Congress and we can do this at our local library.

The next step was convincing the individual teachers to allow tape recording of their lectures, since L.D. people are notoriously poor at note taking. Some allowed recording without hesitation, but others were very upset at the thought, feeling that their teaching skills would somehow be questioned. Of course, we simply wanted the tapes so that the students could listen to each lecture as often as they needed to, but I really began to wonder about some of those teachers. What were they afraid of? Were they ill-prepared?

Another necessary step was the institution of readers for examinations. One must remember that if one is being tested in English literature, the teacher should want to know what the student has learned about English literature, not his reading level. If students are not allowed to demonstrate what they have learned in English literature or algebra, then don't call it English literature or algebra; call it reading. If one's major problem is in reading and one can't understand the questions, how can one ever demonstrate what has been learned? Unless such things are considered, students such as these would find that, for them, the least restrictive environment would be a self-contained L.D. class forever! We professionals can't have it both ways; we can't pay lip service to, "Oh yes, these kids need to be in a social learning environment," unless we also provide the mechanisms for them to be successful in that environment. So often, the only adaptation a school needs to make is to provide a reader for the dyslexic or a writer for the dysgraphic; such a little thing, but for the person with L.D. the difference is between success and constant failure—self-esteem or self-hate.

When Tara was in the fourth grade she had a sensitive and very wise teacher. Tara's writing problems were such that she simply could not finish her work although she learned quickly and communicated well. Her fourth-grade teacher, whom I will always admire, also had in her class a terribly shy little girl, Paula, who had no friends. Paula had beautiful handwriting, so the teacher said, "Paula, you have the prettiest handwriting in the class. Tara has a lot to say, but she has trouble writing. I'm assigning you to be Tara's secretary!" It was marvelous, for Tara and Paula became friends and Paula started to talk. For Tara, suddenly all the things she wanted to write came bubbling forth. The whole experience did not cost the school a penny and gave two little girls a new lease on life. There are many beautiful, creative minds being held back by a pencil.

Daryl was an extremely bright high school student from a caring family that did a particularly fine job of supporting him. School was a different story. The high school was in a university town, and such places usually demand high standards of their teachers, but administrators can make or break a school, and that principal was a very weak man. He provided no leadership, provided minimal inservice for his faculty, and never wished to disturb the status quo. Daryl was dysgraphic, just as Tara was, and he could never finish his tests in the allotted time. On the final examination in English literature, he answered fifty multiple choice questions perfectly, demonstrating that he obviously knew the content. The other 50 percent of the test was essay questions.

Laboriously, he tried to write. He had four sentences down when the time was up. He was failed for the course. Daryl was completely frustrated, furious, and heartbroken, as were his parents. Such treatment of children is totally incomprehensible to me, and it occurs thousands of times every day.

The problem the dyscalculic person faces is different. He often reverses the sequence of numbers, adds or subtracts from left to right, as one would read, rather than from right to left as one should. He can be taught to monitor his errors by a careful teacher. Cathy brought me a sheet of multiplication problems she had completed. She had learned the finger multiplication method, and so she could do the problems, but much of the paper was marked wrong. The problems looked like this:

$$
\begin{array}{r} 9 \\ \times 3 \\ \hline 72 \end{array}
\qquad
\begin{array}{r} 5 \\ \times 3 \\ \hline 51 \end{array}
$$

Obviously, she had written the answers in reverse order, but now she was confused. "I was sure that 3 × 5 was 15!" she said, "But, I guess it's not." "Cathy," I said, "read this number aloud to me." "Fifty-one," she said, then her eyes brightened, "Oh, that's what is wrong!" If her teacher had looked at the problems instead of just checking off right or wrong, she would have noticed that all of Cathy's errors were reversals. If Cathy had read the numerals aloud, she would have known whether she had written them correctly, and the teacher would have realized that Cathy knew the answers. The teacher said she couldn't; it would take too much time.

Multiplication tables are extremely difficult for L.D. children to learn because they are purely a memory task, requiring little thought. One just has to memorize, which is a difficult task for many L.D. people. Persons with learning disabilities tend to do much better with concrete learning that establishes a concept, then progressing from that initial understanding to the more abstract form. Unfortunately, we do not teach that way after about

the second grade, and so children who were only mildly dyscalculic in the beginning may become severely disabled in
adolescence.

Rob was furious at fractions. His inability to do them was
keeping him from the more advanced classes needed for his
major. One day I brought in an apple and a knife. I cut the apple
in half, and said, "Look, Rob, 2, the number on the bottom, is the
number of pieces into which I cut this apple. The number on top,
2, is the number of pieces I have left. When I put the pieces back
together, the number on the bottom stays the same because
that's how many pieces I cut it into. When the number on the top,
2 is the same as the number on the bottom, 2, it equals 1." I then
cut the apple into four pieces. "The number on the bottom is 4
because that's how many pieces I cut it into and the number on
the top is 4 because I still have all the pieces. If I eat one, the
number on the bottom is still 4 because that's how many pieces I
cut, but the number on the top is now 3. When the number on the
top is less than the number on the bottom, I have less than one." I
went on like that for a few minutes.

Rob struck the desk with his fist and cried out in frustration,
"Is that all there is to fractions? Ever since the fifth grade,
they've tried to teach me that and I never learned. Why did I
have to go through all of that?" Do you, the reader, have an answer for him? I don't.

There are many forms of learning disabilities, and many books
to help the psychologist and teacher deal with the different types.
These few types of disabilities mentioned here are included only
to alert the reader to some of the really minor adaptations that
can be implemented with little or no cost to the school or to the
individual, but through them, we can make the difference for our
children. In what other aspect of our lives do we have the opportunity to do such good for others with so little effort?

A major problem for concerned educators is the multicategori-
cal placements in some high schools. In my state, we have a fas-
cinating statistic; virtually half of our L.D. students get well over
the summer between the eighth and ninth grades. Staffed into

L.D. resource rooms in the eighth grade, they are nowhere to be found in the ninth. The reason is the multiple categorical placement where L.D. youngsters are required to attend class with behavior problem students and with the retarded. The class is for the rejected students of the school, or as they are often called, the weirdos or the retards. Because the L.D. students are bright enough to know what's being said, and because most still care what others think of them, they simply will not go. I cannot blame the parents who will not force them; my own children didn't go either.

Even when they first come to college, some will refuse to walk down the hall with me, certain that just by knowing me, others will know about them, that awful secret. Only when they see the other students in the program and see how great they are, are they able to relax and work with us. A few never do.

Another serious problem is the misidentification of children. Too often, I see students who are clearly retarded or emotionally disturbed, who have been labeled learning disabled. In fact, one school principal told me he had never thought of a certain child as being L.D. because she had no behavior problems. It is a common misconception. Another problem is that with increased publicity about famous scientists, artists, olympic stars, and surgeons who were learning disabled, L.D. has become an acceptable label. It is now seen, as it should be, as a disability one can live with. Emotional problems reflect on the family and their parenting skills. Mental retardation projects a limit to one's ability and future life. L.D. is much more acceptable. It is an interesting finding that in my state, the higher the income level of the community and of the immediate family, the fewer children are classified as retarded and emotionally disturbed, and a disproportionate number are labeled L.D. This mislabeling is sad because each disability has different educational needs and what it really means is mistreated children, and a lack of courage, indeed honesty, on the part of school personnel.

A significant problem in education today, and I suspect it will be with us for some time owing to emotional, not educational, factors is this misidentification of children. Some studies of L.D. classrooms have shown that fewer than 50 percent of the children enrolled were actually learning disabled. The other children were most likely to be children with behavior problems or were slow learners or both. This is no simple problem for two very important reasons. First, states vary widely in the criteria they use to determine whether or not a child is learning disabled. Some states use a formula system, where test scores are placed within a formula and placement is determined by a point system. Other states use a discrepancy model, so that a child must be so many years behind his peers before placement can occur. The discrepancy model is particularly unfair to the very young and to the gifted L.D. children. It is hard to get very behind in reading when one is only six years old. If one is gifted, one can often compensate effectively for a while, at least, but never really be challenged in other ways.

The statistical or regression formula model depends upon meaningful test scores, yet any good clinician knows that L.D. cannot help but influence test scores. This formula is also basically designed to look for severe discrepancies. Yet the number of children identified as learning disabled has skyrocketed since Public Law 94–142 was passed, while school enrollment has declined. The overidentification of so-called L.D. children is really misidentification in many cases. The major problems are inadequate assessment tools, or tests; no standard battery of tests, even within the same school district; and placement decisions based on factors other than assessment.

The second major factor is perhaps more defensible, yet no less serious a consideration than the first. The most used IQ tests in the nation are the Weschler scales. These tests use a range of 90–110 as a normal, or average, IQ score. The standard deviation from the mean of 100 is 15 points. In some states, if a child's score is more than 15 points below the mean, or 84 points, the child is classed as a slow learner, not L.D. In other states, the cutoff is two standard deviations, or 30 or more points below average. Any teacher knows the difference in teaching a child with a 70 IQ versus teaching a child with a 100 IQ, yet they are often in the same L.D. classroom.

This situation has come about because of a basic disagreement among some professionals. Simply put, there are those who believe that learning disabilities can occur in children with low IQ's. There are others who believe that mental retardation is one handicapping condition and that learning disabilities is another; that they are separate conditions requiring different educational treatment. Parents, too, prefer an L.D. label for their children for the reasons already stated. For many, the problem crystalizes when they look for a college program for the child they have come to think of as L.D. I know of no college L.D. program that knowingly accepts slow learners. It is simply not fair to place them in college curricula when they are certain to fail.

What other things can we do, as educators, to ensure the success we want for all of our students? Teachers can't change their room, the number of students, or the curriculum they teach, but they can change their mode of presentation. The best teachers are the most flexible ones, adapting their presentations to the various learning styles of the students. To learn what these styles are, a teacher should present their students with something to learn and instruct them to learn it any way they want to. By making it fun, giving the students some outrageous options, the teacher can determine how they learned it. The next topic should be taught that way.

People know how they learn best although they may not be aware of it. Look around you in any learning situation. Some people will be taking prodigious notes, others will sit quietly just listening. If teachers pay attention to their students, they will learn from them. Most L.D. people can also explain how they learn best. My daughter puts her head down on her desk and listens with her eyes shut. She doesn't overload visually that way, and she can recite, practically verbatim, what the professors have said. It is the way, we are told, that General George S. Patton got through West Point. Her putting her head down bothers some professors, even when she's explained why she does it, but what is she to do, stare at them and not learn? Teachers must accept their students' differences, and really do what we've been talking about for years—individualize instruction as much as possible. No, what some of you are thinking impossible is possible. With 144 students each day in my high school English classes, I've done it. One can lecture sometimes, have small groups, and so on. One is limited only by one's imagination. Assign one paper for content only; correct no grammar or spelling and tell your students you won't. You will be surprised at the beautiful, creative minds being held back by spelling problems and dictionaries. Grade the next paper for grammar and spelling, and average the grades! Try it just once, and you won't go back to the old way.

A major problem for most L.D. students is a lack of organization. It is not that they have little to say, it is that they do not know how to organize it, or indeed, even how to begin. At Achieve, we teach a student to write one fact or one statement on one note card. When the information is collected, we put three pieces of paper on a table. One is labeled Introduction; the next, Body; the third, Conclusion. We have the students place each note card on the paper on which it belongs. Body and Conclusion are put aside and the student begins with Introduction. Through understanding the organization, the student usually can complete the paper with little outside help.

Buy the *How to Spell It* book, in which all the ways a word might be spelled are listed in one color and the correct way is in another color. Remember, you can't look up a word in the dictionary if you don't know how to spell it! Our own president, Andrew Jackson, stated that it was a damn poor mind that could think of only one way to spell a word. I call my students "creative spellers." When all teachers realize that almost all people with L.D. can function in a regular classroom with minor adaptations such as untimed testing, tape recorders, or presenting papers orally, then schools will finally move forward in the education of all their students. An L.D. teacher said to me of her student, "He reads with his ears and he writes with his mouth." And that's all right. Many business executives function in just that way, by listening and dictating.

Making these adaptations insures success. It is not unfair to the other students. It is an adaptation while a person needs it, just as we might need a crutch while a broken leg is healing. One of my students, angry at his treatment by educators, said that if he could say one thing to teachers, it would be: "Forget fair or unfair—educate! It's not a contest! Teach! That's your job!" And indeed it is.

A word must be said for teachers, too. Working with a person with L.D. is not always rewarding. One gives one's best, only to receive little feedback, only to be tossed aside. No one who works with the learning disabled is immune from hurt. Parents fuss at you even when you're doing your darndest to help their child, and students may not appreciate you either. It is a normal feeling at times to say to oneself, "If they don't care, why should I?"

Ann was a super student, conscientious to a fault, at times. Because of a physical problem, she had been closely watched. She was her mother's baby, and she became extremely upset at any possible scholastic problem. Ann's solution to any problem was to call her mother, who rushed to her aid. I had a mental picture of Mrs. X on her white charger going out to do battle with the latest dragon. When Ann wanted to go on to graduate school, the latest dragon became Ann's tutor of three years, Ellen.

Ellen had been Ann's tutor, first as an Achieve member, and later, without pay, for another two years. She loved her, thought they were friends. Ann was about to take the exams she would need to enter graduate school, and Ellen had been tutoring her; Ann would need extended time and a special proctor to read for her. Without mentioning it to Ellen, Ann wrote a letter to testing services, volunteering Ellen for the nine-hour testing. Later, she told Ellen, who expressed surprise. Ellen, newly married, knew her husband would not be thrilled at her being away on the one day each week they had together, and she was not at all sure the testing service would allow her to proctor a student she had tutored. Assuring Ann that she would never let her down, Ellen left to call the proctoring service. Even that expression of surprise roused alarms in Ann's head, and true to form, she called her mother. Her mother immediately called the proctoring service, complaining that the person they had lined up to do the proctoring had backed out, criticizing Ellen by name. She then jumped in her car to save the day. In the meantime, the service called Ellen and said she could not proctor, just as she had suspected. Before Ellen could reach Ann, Ann and her mother met Ellen's new husband and gave him a check to pay Ellen off. Fifteen dollars for three years; never had Ellen requested payment, not even for the gas to get to tutoring sessions, hard to come by on a student's salary.

Ellen was deeply hurt. Finally, she wrote Ann, explaining her feelings and calling her on her behavior, because, for our students' sakes, we cannot allow such behavior to continue. Ultimately, to ignore such behavior would be the greater cruelty, but that doesn't stop it from hurting. To her credit, Ann eventually called to apologize.

We teachers chose this field. We will not always be appreciated, but that never excuses us from being the best that we can be. If we were to do what we're supposed to do, we would have *Typing Keys* classes for the learning disabled in our schools in place of the regular typing classes in which they fail. We would have their books on tape so that they can learn the content while we are teaching them to read according to their modality preference in the resource room. We would identify them intelligently. We would allow them to dictate into a tape recorder that which they cannot get down on paper. We would test them orally, reading the questions to them if need be, so that we could determine what they have learned in that class rather than the speed with which they can write it. We would institute training so that teachers and students understand that *dyslexic* doesn't mean retarded, that all people learn differently, but that most all can learn. We would have a class in the high school that teaches what L.D. is and is not, so that the L.D. students and others can learn what is right with them instead of only what is wrong. We would have a class in interpersonal skills, video-taping ourselves and the students in such areas as job applications, interviews, and telephoning. We would teach them about eye contact, a firm handshake, body language, and communication. In other words, we would educate.

At a party, a university professor overheard me discussing my program. Later, he asked if we could go someplace as he needed to talk. He told me of his dyslexia, of his skills at dictation, and how he had hidden this "defect" at what cost for so long. He told me how he and his best friend had once partied into the night, and how he had "confessed" his dyslexia to his friend. Upon awakening, he was so ashamed that he didn't speak to his friend for two weeks. He said these things to me in a hoarse whisper and the whole impression was that he was confessing to some murderous act, instead of a problem with reading. This man is highly successful, the winner of many government grants, an author. We taught him that he is unworthy; we taught him to be so ashamed.

We should be ashamed.

8

ALL THAT I DESERVE
JUVENILE DELINQUENCY AND L.D.

In recent years, through the joint efforts of the Association for Children and Adults with Learning Disabilities and the federal government, the correlation between learning disabilities and juvenile delinquency has been examined. The results of this research, studies from France and Great Britain, as well as studies conducted by state and other agencies in the United States, are consistent in their results. There is a correlation between learning disabilities and juvenile delinquency. Furthermore, the correlation between school failure, caused by reading problems in particular, and juvenile delinquency is much greater than the impact on the child of the socioeconomic level of his family.

Research has shown that 80 percent of the juvenile delinquents do not have life plans; yet that statistic drops to only 11 percent if the person receives his high school diploma, General Educational Development (G.E.D.) certificate or even finishes a vocational program.

We know that the juvenile delinquent is most likely to come from a single parent home; he is often abused; he has rarely seen an optometrist, a dentist, or a physician. His parents did not provide food, housing, or clothes on a regular basis. Although the majority of the learning disabled have had those advantages, they perhaps share a problem with the typical juvenile delinquent. As one said so succinctly to me, "I couldn't read the book, so I shut it and hit the street, 'cause out there, he don't know and I don't know, so we've got something in common. You put a bunch of nothings together—you've got trouble. At school, I just built a barrier around myself."

To fit comfortably into a society, one must believe in the values of that society. There must be an attachment and involvement in the community. Because of the way he has often been treated, it is easy to understand why the L.D. delinquent's feelings of detachment from society have occurred, and because he feels detached the rules of society have less importance for him. Laws are for other people, not necessarily for him. What, after all, has society given him? When one is valued or devalued in the eyes of one's society, there is a tendency to live up to, or down to, the expectations of that society. We all know people who, because of someone's belief in them, have become more successful than others ever thought they would be. We also know others who seem to drift along, making little investment in society or in themselves; or else they choose a subculture of society, such as the drug scene, delinquency, or both.

Some adolescents are unsuccessful in developing peer relationships and feel isolated. While all teenagers feel isolated sometimes, it is the constant rejection and isolation these children feel that often causes them to turn to drugs. Peer relationships are not luxuries; they are necessities.

Although there is no specific type of adolescent who uses marijuana or amphetamines, he tends to be middle class. Those who abuse alcohol usually have parents who are heavy drinkers. Heroin users tend to come more from poor inner city neighborhoods, broken homes, and racial minority groups. Those who tend to abuse these substances are generally people who have suffered a disruption of normal parent-child relationships; a lack of involvement with organized groups, such as church or scouts; and who lack good peer interactions.

Other factors are also implicated. Low verbal intelligence, arrest record of a parent, erratic or lax supervision by a parent, crowded, broken, or disorderly home, and indifference or hostility of parent(s) are serious problems for any child. For the child on the way to delinquency, each factor is another step in the wrong direction.

The period of a person's life between the ages of twelve and seventeen is the time of the greatest division between the child and his society. As of this writing, the average age of first confrontation as a delinquent is twelve and a half years. Those adolescent years are a period of greater anxiety than most parents realize. Instinctively, the adolescent begins to draw away from his family as a part of growing up and developing the independence he will need later. Acceptance by his peer group allows this withdrawal to occur without the loneliness he would otherwise feel, for we all need to belong to something or to somebody. Sadly, it is often this critical component that is missing in the life of the L.D. person.

Although those with learning disabilities can come from all walks of life, the majority of those with learning disabilities who become delinquent do not come from abusive homes any more than they come from economically deprived ones. They drifted into delinquent behavior for other, but no less important, reasons. There is a tendency to want immediate gratification among the learning disabled. Perhaps difficulties in time and space relationships do not give the L.D. person a method to judge how long one must wait to receive a reward; it must seem safer to get it now. Therefore, if he wants the latest popular album, it's better to take it today rather than wait until he has saved up enough money to buy it later. If he is caught, in society's eyes, he is delinquent.

Learning disabled people often have difficulties in determining the effects of their actions. Pam jumped on a frog, killing it instantly, and then was heartbroken at its death. She had not thought through what the result of her action would be and was genuinely distressed when it happened. In many L.D. people, there is the tendency to plunge ahead without thought of the consequences. To those of us who see ahead and therefore control our actions, such behavior is difficult to understand.

Sometimes it seems that they are heedless of the feelings and needs of others. There is a tendency among this group to be so involved with their own feelings and desires that those of others are not even considered. They may then be seen by others, even those who love them the most, as thoughtless, uncaring people.

Poor impulse control is expressed in demanding gratification immediately, interrupting without thought, engaging in behavior without thinking of the consequences, the inability to stick to a task until it is finished, and so forth. These kinds of behaviors are difficult to live with and difficult for educators to deal with.

When an adolescent is actually caught in the commission of a crime, how he responds to the initial questioning of the policeman has an impact on how he is subsequently treated. The verbally astute, nonhandicapped peer who took the car for a brief joy-ride is usually more adept at talking his way out of a situation. If he is arrested, he is more likely to be able to explain his behavior, express his sorrow over the act, and therefore please the authorities. The L.D. person lacking these skills is statistically more likely to be arrested initially and to be actually charged with the offense than is his nonhandicapped peer, even though both committed the identical delinquent act. When he faces a judge, he will not receive a stiffer sentence, perhaps because of more specific guidelines regarding sentences.

As a group, L.D. males are more likely to perform delinquent acts, such as theft, or those acts which are destructive and violent against property or people, whereas L.D. females are more likely to indulge in petty theft, such as shoplifting, and in overt sexual activities. Interestingly, delinquency is proportionately higher in the group of L.D. children from families with higher educational and occupational levels, than in L.D. children from lower socioeconomic levels. We must, therefore, ask ourselves if a component of their delinquency is the inability to live up to the educational and socioeconomic goals of their families.

It has often been stated that when a person feels helpless to change a situation, one of two behaviors will develop. The first is aggression. Aggression is a common result when people are made to feel helpless and hopeless. Some of us get really angry over things we can't control, so we slam doors or kick a chair. We may take out our anger at the boss on our spouse or children. Such aggression begins as verbal abuse, but too many cases of physical abuse occur for it to be ignored.

The point is, that when we feel powerless to change a situation that we want very much to change, we often strike out. One of my students became so angry at his father's continual demands that he struck the mirror with his fist, shattering it and mangling his hand. Another picked a fight and lost a front tooth. There has to be an outlet for feelings of worthlessness. Often, it appears in destructive acts against ourselves or others.

It has been suggested that when real problems exist, they proceed sequentially; the individual experiences repeated school failure; school becomes a place he detests, so he refuses to go; he becomes a truant; given the free time he now has, he is easy prey for those who wish to include him in their delinquent acts. Easily led and eager to be a member of a group, any group, he willingly accepts them and joins their acts, accepts their behavior, and adopts their values. While the process has been simplified, it is still the down-to-earth, bottom line of the problem.

Cal was big for his age. At twelve, he was over six feet tall, slightly overweight, and had a bad case of acne. His parents had immigrated from a European country and their native language was still the language of the home. Cal wanted to be like the kids in his class, so he rejected the native language and never spoke in that tongue.

He didn't do well in school because reading and spelling were impossible tasks for him. Every night, his father, a great bear of a man, would place Cal upon his lap, clouds of strong cigar smoke surrounding them, and force Cal to read from the family Bible. Many years later, as his father lay dying from cancer of the throat, Cal brought him a slate so he could write down what he wanted to say. The father looked at Cal with tears in his eyes and said, "I cannot write, I cannot read." All those years of pretending; "Read, Cal!" The child, turned man, understood at last.

At the time, though, there had been much bitterness. Cal hated school. He couldn't tell time, so he carved on his desk the place where the hands of the clock would be when school was out.

He was the only one he knew who consistently fell up the stairs. When he was a school crossing guard, he fell over the pole that held the flag so many times that his father finally made one out of a broom handle, which couldn't be broken. Then, when he fell, only Cal was hurt; the flag stayed intact. Socially, Cal wasn't doing well either. Even though he became a handsome man, as an adolescent he was big and awkward; he didn't fit in. As an adult, one of his most painful memories was of a dinner dance during those teen years.

Perhaps because of his size, people expected more of him than they had a right to. Inside, he felt very small and out of place. The only people who wanted him around was the gang at the corner. Cal was smart and big, as well. He understood the principle of a lever, so when the gang wanted to tip over the tombstones in the cemetery, Cal knew just how to do it. When someone wanted to throw a Molotov cocktail at a bus, Cal knew how to make one. He never thought up these acts, nor did he give a thought to the consequences, but at last he was a valued, trusted member of a group. He was a hair's-breadth away from a life of crime.

Cal was saved because of a teacher, who somehow saw the potential in a rapidly developing delinquent. She kept him busy, hiring him to paint cabinets that didn't need painting; hiring him to carry material to workshops in other parts of the state, exposing him to another world of success and opportunity. Finally, at seventeen, his father got him a job in the steel mill where he worked, operating a machine that had already killed two men. Cal couldn't stand it anymore, so he forged his parents' signatures and enlisted in the Army. When his father found out, he knocked him across the room.

All of the factors were in place for the development of antisocial behavior; a difficult family situation, school failure, low self-concept; yet in Cal's case it never really materialized. Cal went on to complete a doctorate, though it took him double the number of years that it should have taken him to receive it. Still, it was accomplished. Some of his old friends are still in jail. What made the difference?

When Tina was in third grade, she was staffed into an L.D. resource room for part of the day. She was a gifted learning disabled student with an IQ above 140, genius level. She could read anything, but her math skills were very weak and her handwriting was atrocious. Spelling was a major concern. Tina was a typical dyscalculic and dysgraphic child, common forms of learning disabilities, although not as well known as dyslexia, the reading disability. Her L.D. teacher was pleasant and caring, but she lacked the knowledge of how to help Tina. She made ditto sheets; each had only one math problem on it, in huge numerals, "like they had for retarded kids," Tina said. Tina rebelled. Her math skills weren't that low, she just couldn't memorize the multiplication tables, so she wrote the answers to the problems in the smallest print she could make, in the lower corner of the page. In that way, she became a rebellious child in the minds of the school, and spent much of that year in the hall. Things didn't improve. Although she came from a loving home and was a cherished child, her parents were having problems of their own and eventually divorced.

Tina moved with her mother and siblings to another town, where a well-meaning but ignorant teacher told the other students in the junior high class that Tina couldn't help it, but there was something a little wrong with her brain and they should be good to her. Thereafter, no one would have anything to do with Tina. Her mother took time off from work to go on field trips with the class so Tina would not be so alone. Tina was the youngest child and her brothers and sisters were involved with their own lives. Her mother had to work to support them, and so Tina was forced to spend a lot of time alone.

When she got to high school, the undeserved reputation followed her. School was a constant problem; teachers could not understand how this intelligent, articulate girl could fail every written test. They told her she was lazy. Eventually, Tina gave up trying. As friends, she sought out those who were rejected. Easily led, she followed along with another's plan and was picked up for shoplifting and placed on probation. She wrecked the family car twice and remained convinced that it wasn't her fault, although she received tickets both times. The resulting financial and emotional strains on the family were terrible. Her siblings couldn't understand her behavior, showing open disapproval, and her mother was devastated. Tina felt helpless, but so did they.

She was becoming an attractive young woman, yet she chose as a boyfriend one who was both verbally and physically abusive. Did she feel that was all she deserved? When her mother, in desperation, tried to warn her about him, Tina ran away from home. It could have gone either way at that point. Fortunately, for all involved, her mother sent her to a private L.D. school, where her self-concept improved drastically. As she began to have more confidence in her own abilities, others began to treat her differently. Encouraged, she enrolled in a college which had L.D. support services, broke up with the boyfriend, and found a new boyfriend who was caring. She began to love life again and continues to do well. But society could have lost her; we lose so many.

Even when things begin to improve, it may not be possible for the adolescent to believe it. When the principal announced at the high school graduation that Pat had won the most improved student award, Pat went out in the parking lot and broke the principal's car windows with a baseball bat. Hating what had happened to him academically, hating the principal's reference to it, even in a complimentary manner, hating himself, Pat made certain that others would see him as he felt himself to be; a bad kid.

It is obvious to judges, teachers, and parents that the behavior of Cal, Tina, Pat, and all the others is self-destructive. It must be understood that the learning disabled person does not necessarily see it that way. His behavior is filling a need, a need for acceptance by somebody just as he is. After having been told over and over that he is a failure, lazy, and stupid, his life becomes a self-fulfilling prophecy—I am no good, therefore I'll act that way. I am worthless, so what does it matter what I do? I will associate with those whom I perceive to be as worthless as I.

Kitty chose a different path. A disproportionate number of adolescents who are learning disabled exhibit substance abuse, drugs, or more often in my experience, alcohol. Kitty used both. By fourteen, she skipped school more often than she attended. She was a pretty girl, who with less makeup would have been lovely. Her major outlet was sexual. It was easy to find someone to tell her she was pretty and desirable. At last, as she said, she had found "something she could do."

It was not until her parents placed her in an institution as an incorrigible child at seventeen that the psychiatrist discovered her learning disabilities. Kitty tried after that to get her life together, and she would succeed for a month or two. Despite placement in a school that tried to meet her needs, and parents who tried to help and support her, Kitty could not sustain the effort and she would go on a two- or three-day drinking binge during which she would go home with any man who asked her to. Her parents have told her she can't come home again. I am fearful of her future, for today, at twenty-two, she is full of self-hate.

Although each of these cases represents real people and the problems they have gone through because of their actions, there is another group of the learning disabled who seem to become delinquents almost by accident. Gary side-swiped a car and was given a ticket and a court appearance date. He forgot to go, so he was cited for contempt of court and assigned another court date, which he also forgot. He was fined one thousand dollars and given another court date. He eventually had to take a year off from college to earn the money to pay the fine and his lawyer.

Even more benign was Tom's case. Tom got a speeding ticket. He was not at all concerned; everybody gets a speeding ticket sometimes, don't they? When he received two more tickets, his driver's license was revoked. He continued to drive, and as usual, too fast. When he had received nine tickets, he was sent to jail, still loudly protesting that everybody gets speeding tickets. Of course, his parents are devastated at having their son in jail and are astounded at his lack of judgment.

Forgetting really important dates, even pleasant ones, is a common practice in L.D. people. One of my students won a state art contest, and forgot to go to the ceremony to receive his prize.

The lack of judgment, in so many areas, is also very common among people with L.D., with often disastrous results for themselves and their loved ones. Cause and effect—what will happen to you if you do not follow nature's or society's laws—often seem to escape them.

A word must be said for parents. We wear out. When our children are constantly in trouble, we are embarrassed and ashamed because others know about this child who will not conform. We ask ourselves what we did wrong, and what could we have done differently? Guilt and anguish weigh heavily upon us, and every parent can remember something about which he wishes he had been wiser.

When our own value systems are challenged by our child's behavior, we are forced to decide how to deal with it. Your daughter, at eighteen, moves in with a man. Your son quits school to follow some girl around the country, and like the prodigal son comes home only when he's out of money. Your child deliberately injures animals. Your child, who lives at home, refuses to abide by your rules, coming in at all hours stoned on drugs or drunk. I find few things sadder than a parent who tells me he just wishes his child would go away so that the family could have some peace. One father even told me that he believed in reincarnation, and so if his son wanted to destroy himself, let him. His mother was not willing to give up on him, though. We cannot be. We need to continue to love him, not the behavior, and to remember that nonhandicapped children get into trouble, too. There are degrees of misbehavior, from a level of rebelliousness to outright disobedience. All teenagers are defiant to some extent. Suggestions from parents are often unwelcome. Rejection of parental values may take the form of verbal arguments and failure to conform. The adolescent wants his style of dress, his music, his friends, his extracurricular activities, and the freedom to choose these without any help from his parents. What to one set of parents is out-of-control behavior, to another set of parents may be nothing more than some teenage hijinks. Behavior must therefore be considered in the context of the value system of the family. Each of us must decide what behavior we can accept and what we can live with. The family of the boy who broke all the rules decided to lock the door at 1:00 a.m. When they could live with his behavior no longer, they rented a room at the Y.M.C.A. for him. These are terribly painful decisions.

Even though a correlation between juvenile delinquency and learning disabilities has been shown to exist, it must be remembered that even among the socially disabled, most students aren't delinquent. For those who are and their families, heartache is a constant companion.

What can you do? Get help, for yourselves and your child, if he will go. If he won't, and I've had some clients run away from me, at least get help for yourselves in dealing with your child's behavior. Family counseling for the other family members is often necessary, too, for they are as upset and embarrassed as you are. Brothers and sisters are mortified and ashamed.

Some parents hesitate to seek help because of their shame. You need to remember that you aren't going to tell the psychologist anything she or he hasn't heard before, and, by oath, the psychologist cannot reveal what you discuss to anyone. Find someone with whom you feel comfortable and talk it through. It's very hard to find your own solutions when you are so emotionally involved in the situation. Remember also that those suggestions about taking some form of action discussed in chapter 4 can make all the difference in how well your family copes with your problems.

Try to set up only those rules that you think must be absolute, then follow through on them. Try not to nag about haircuts, makeup, or clothes, saving your strength for really important issues. As my father has often said, "Don't use your shotgun on a mosquito."

As parents, try not to blame one another or the child. That is water under the bridge. We have to deal with what is happening now, and who did what, when, only hurts family togetherness. You need each other now as you never have before.

Never tell children that they are bad or evil. Tell them you hate the act or the behavior, but never the person. You can never say

"I love you" too often, to anyone. Adolescent L.D.'s have sometimes been amazed at what they have done, but being teenagers also, they have serious trouble admitting it, especially to their parents. Sometimes they have known exactly what they were doing, but were so angry with themselves and with society that they did it anyway. Try to understand/remember that they do not like themselves either. They know their behavior is not acceptable and will accomplish nothing but more rejection, which nobody really wants.

Most learning disabled adolescents will not turn into adult criminals. Cling to that while you're hurting, and for all your sakes, don't give up.

9 NOBODY EVER TALKS ABOUT CHARLES
WHERE DO WE GO FROM HERE?

"Nobody ever talks about Charles," the woman said wistfully. It was not a criticism, it was a statement of fact, which startled me. I was surprised because I had just finished a speech about learning disabled adults and I had really tried to cover as much of the topic as I could, therefore her remark caught my immediate attention and I thought long about it, for she was right.

As professionals, we report data, try to teach other professionals what techniques have worked for our students, and try to help parents deal with their L.D. children more effectively. With parents in particular, we try to be very upbeat, talking in positive ways about upbringing and future goals. It's a sort of "Hang in there; this too shall pass" approach. Happily, for most parents it does get better, but there are a few for whom it does not, not for themselves, not for their children.

The older adult with learning disabilities who has not received adequate help is often an alien in a world which values achievers. Those who are now in their late twenties and thirties who still live at home, who work at menial jobs, are the Charles of whom the mother spoke. When he is out of school, there are very few places where he can go to receive treatment.

We know that the identified learning disabled person who is still at home in these later years tends to lack job skills, to have lower functioning levels, and tends to lack those social skills that would allow him to advance in society. As one parent put it, "He is always permanent, temporary help. He may stay at the same menial job for many years, but he will be the first to be fired. He will never receive benefits because he is temporary help. All this means that he cannot earn enough money to live on his own even if he had the skills, so he must always live with us."

I find, too, that his parents are older, and often tired of fighting for this child in an adult body. As one father said, "When I buy two rocking chairs, I'll just buy three." Because many L.D. adults have high medical bills, this continued dependence can be financially devastating for older parents, who must continue to carry their child on their medical insurance policy, which may no longer be in effect once the parents retire.

Maybe the parents looked forward to retiring in a trailer to some sunny spot by a lake. They can't do that now, and they can't have those lovely, carefree years alone either.

Parents have to worry about what will happen to this child should they become ill or when they die. Where will he go? Who will take care of him? Brothers and sisters are often unwilling to accept into their homes another adult who is sure to disrupt their lives.

These concerns, and all the others, are fair and honest. These are real problems which real people face. No, it isn't fair that you should have these worries. No, it isn't fair that your neighbor can move to Sun City and you cannot. No, it isn't fair that your retirement years, for which you've worked so long, cannot be carefree. Having established that it isn't fair, we are right back to the beginning statements in this book, get busy.

Often, the easiest way to begin is to interest the person in a specific skill, such as sailing. Go with him to the sailing club meeting, learn about different boat classes, regattas, rigging. As he learns, he will have something else to talk about to people who have the same interests and will be less inclined to withdraw into himself. Psychologically, it is also much healthier.

Convince your L.D. person to volunteer. Getting out of oneself is critical. A good way to begin is to care for someone else. The person with L.D. should start in a nonthreatening place, such as volunteering for playground duty or helping the little ones with their work. Many schools have active volunteer programs, and volunteers at hospitals and Senior Citizens' homes are usually sought. People are lonely and someone to wheel them around the grounds or just to talk to are such welcome visitors. We grow out of ourselves by doing something for someone else, and because people love to talk about themselves, those whose company is most sought out are those who are the best listeners. The L.D. person who doesn't like to talk can develop into a terrific listener.

Joining an environmental club, such as the Audubon Society or the Sierra Club, whatever one believes in, can be a great outlet. Such clubs always need volunteers, to stuff envelopes, even, but every interaction will teach, and one is safe with people who believe in the same issues; and how involved the volunteer becomes depends on him.

People with learning disabilities are often very self-conscious about the way they appear to others, they need to be taught appropriate behavior. One of the best ways is through drama. We often read about the use of the "arts" to teach handicapped people, but art and music are what are usually meant by the "arts." Theatre is often ignored, and yet, as Dr. Sylvia Richardson has said, the theatre can provide an excellent forum for teaching social skills. Consider. When one is playing a part, the director speaks to the individual as the character he is portraying, not the person he really is. For instance, "Sam would be very interested in what the doctor is saying at this point. Look at his face and listen carefully to what he is saying." The director is teaching how one should respond in a very nonthreatening manner, for he is saying what the character, Sam, should do, not the real person. Or, "She has been threatened," or "She has received some exciting news," "Her response would be . . ." Most directors show their actors how their bodies and faces should respond and what the word emphasis should be for that character. Such criticism is acceptable to the L.D. person because it is not really directed at him personally but to the character he portrays.

In addition, the drama exposes one to all the vagaries of life in a vicarious way, so one can see how others solve their problems and can measure the results of these actions. Ideally, a person who knows the theatre and understands L.D.ness would be the perfect director. The Achieve Program at Southern Illinois University has begun such a group, but one can always join a little theatre group in the community.

Most little theatre groups have classes for beginning actors that teach a person how to sit and walk on a stage. Theatre people tend to be very accepting of others' behavior, and because everyone else is learning, too, it is a much less frightening experience.

For those who feel they simply could not get on a stage, ever, there are many other roles within a little theatre company. There are many jobs to be done: sets need to be built, lighting set up, programs handed out, costumes and props prepared—all require many hands.

For those who don't have this opportunity, Patsy Fordyce of the Association for Children with Learning Disabilities suggests that the L.D. person watch soap operas with the sound turned off to help learn how people's bodies and facial expressions indicate their feelings.

Another efficient method of teaching the social skills noted in these chapters is through the use of video taping. A situation is presented, such as a job interview, with the counselor acting the role of interviewer and the L.D. person assuming the role of the job seeker. The interaction is taped, and is viewed immediately afterwards by both participants. This enables the person with L.D. to see himself as others see him and enables the L.D. specialist to stop the tape or run it over and over to point out the behavior that might keep a person from being hired. Situations such as social interaction at a party, appropriate behavior in restaurants, and asking someone out, are easily improved through role playing. Most schools and many families have the necessary equipment.

The types of problems our adults have are varied. Many L.D. adults do not know how to dress appropriately, but there are some lovely little books, listed in the reference section, which teach color coordination and other such skills. One clever adult hired a retired store owner to help her shop, to coordinate her clothes and shoes, and to develop outfits with interchangeable parts. She always looks lovely now.

Many L.D. adults have dreadful problems with fine motor coordination, and so such things as clipping one's nails or using a curling iron are impossible tasks. A parent, teacher, counselor, or friend might take such a person to the hairdresser and help her choose an easy-to-care-for hair style. A friend's feet always hurt because clipping her nails was so difficult. She now gets pedicures.

Those of us who know how to solve such problems as these must share that information. We often just don't think about it.

National conventions of the Association of Children and Adults with Learning Disabilities (A.C.L.D.) and the Orton Society often have speakers who tell parents how to plan their estates for their handicapped children. They have speakers from the rehabilitation programs that detail how job skills are taught at their facilities. Lawyers, advocates for the handicapped, cover a wide range of options and opportunities regarding the lives of the adult population. Parent groups may outline the programs they have in their communities for their adult children, how these programs work, and what they try to accomplish.

If a parent or teacher cannot go to a national conference, they can call the National A.C.L.D. or Orton headquarters, for many of the training sessions are available on tape at minimal cost. Contact state and local associations too, to suggest programs on these topics. Teachers can, and should, be a resource for parents, and tell them about such options.

Parents and teachers need to develop guidelines for themselves and their L.D. people to follow, outlining some of the steps they must follow on the road to independence. These should include:

I. Financial Management
   A. Checking accounts
   B. Credit cards
   C. Earning and spending responsibly
II. Living with Others

 A. Immediate family
  1. communication
  2. taking responsibility
  3. dating/sex education
  4. developing independence
  5. resolving conflicts
 B. Dormitory living
  1. roommates/peers
  2. taking responsibility
  3. resolving conflicts
 C. Apartment living
  1. living alone
   a. organization
   b. shopping
   c. paying bills
  2. living together
   a. setting rules
   b. organization
   c. allocating responsibilities
   d. resolving conflicts
 D. Group home
  1. setting rules
  2. organization
  3. allocating responsibilities
  4. resolving conflicts

Help them to realize that there are options for them. If reading remains a problem, order books on tape from the Library of Congress. If they can't add well, then develop skill with a calculator. Help them to develop conversational skills by talking to them and by providing the feedback mentioned before. In other words, help them to develop a lifestyle as close to that of others as is humanly possible.

When I was working my way through college, I worked at Gimbels' department store one summer. There was a woman in my training group whose face was badly scarred from burns. At first

I noticed the scars, but after we became friends, it surprised me to notice others looking at her, for I no longer saw the disfigurement. I saw only my friend.

So it must be with the learning disabled. We must stop seeing just the disability and see the people. My friend's scars were visible; those of the learning disabled are not, but they are no less painful. Admitting, then, that the scars remain, we need to continue to move forward, to develop new programs. Somebody needs to "talk about Charles," for Tara was right: they were all her sisters; they were all her brothers.

READING MATERIALS, RESIDENTIAL PROGRAMS / CAREER TRAINING, INFORMATION SOURCES

READING MATERIALS, RESIDENTIAL PROGRAMS / CAREER TRAINING, INFORMATION SOURCES

READING MATERIALS

PARENTING

"A Survival Manual: Case Studies and Suggestions for the L.D.
   Teenager"
   Weiss, Helen and Martin
   Tree House Associates, 1981
   Great Barrington, Massachussetts
"Counseling Parents of Exceptional Children"
   Jack C. Stewart
   Charles E. Merrill Publishing Company, 1978
   Columbus, Ohio 43216
"Learning Disabilities: The Struggle from Adolescence Toward
   Adulthood"
   Cruickshank, W. et al.
   Syracuse University Press, 1980
   Syracuse, New York
"No Easy Answers"
   Sally Smith
   Bantam Books, 1979
"Parents as Partners in Education"
   Eugenia Hepworth Berger, Ph.D.
   The C.V. Mosby Company, 1981
   11830 Westline Industrial Drive
   St. Louis, Missouri 63141
"Parent Effectiveness Training"
   Dr. Thomas Cordon

Van Rees Press, 1972
New York, New York
"Parents Speak Out"
Ann P. Turnbull, H. Rutherford Turnbull III
Charles E. Merrill Publishing Company, 1978
Columbus, Ohio 43216
"Parenting Strategies and Educational Methods"
John O. Cooper, Denzil Edge
Charles E. Merrill Publishing Company, 1978
Columbus, Ohio 43216
"Something's Wrong with My Child"
Brutten, Richardson, and Mangel
Harcourt, Brace, Jovanovich, 1973
New York, New York
"On Being the Parent of a Handicapped Youth"
N.Y.A.L.D.
155 Washington Avenue
Albany, New York 12210
"The Powerful Parent: A Child Advocacy Handbook"
D. Gottesman
Appleton-Century-Crofts
Norwalk, Connecticut

SOCIALIZATION

"Learning Disabilities: A Family Affair"
Betty Osman
Random House, 1978
"No One To Play With: The Social Side of Learning Disabilities"
Betty Osman
Random House, 1982
"Learning Disabilities and Human Sexuality"
M. Wood, 1985
Academic Therapy, 20, pp. 543–547

"Social Skills Assessment and Training for the Learning
Disabled. Who's on First and What's on Second?"
Journal of Learning Disabilities, 17, pp. 422–431, 1984
"Training L.D. Students to Cope with the Every Day World"
E. Minskoff, 1982
Academic Therapy, 17, pp. 311–316

JUVENILE DELINQUENCY

"Adolescents with Behavior Problems: Strategies for Teaching,
Counseling, and Parent Involvement"
Vernon F. Jones
Allyn and Bacon, Inc., 1980
470 Atlantic Avenue
Boston, Massachussetts 02210
"Children in Conflict"
Henry R. Reinert
The C.V. Mosby Company, 1976
St. Louis, Missouri
"Delinquent Youth and Learning Disabilities"
Nancy P. Ramos
Academic Therapy Publications, 1978
1539 Fourth Street
San Rafael, California 94901
"Learning Disabilities: Its Implications to a Responsible
Society"
Edited by Doreen Kronick
Academic Therapy Publications, 1974
1539 Fourth Street
San Rafael, California 94901
"Youth in Trouble"
Betty Lou Kratoville, Editor
Academic Therapy Publications, 1975
1539 Fourth Street
San Rafael, California 94901

"A Study Investigating the Link Between Learning Disabilities
and Juvenile Delinquency"
A.C.L.D.–R & D Project Summary
Dorothy Crawford, Project Director
July, 1982
"Where Do We Go from Here?"
Journal of Learning Disabilities
M. Skar
United Way

COLLEGE PROGRAMS

"A Guide to Post-secondary Educational Opportunities for the
Learning Disabled"
Diane Ridenour, Jane Johnston
Time Out To Enjoy, Inc., 1980
715 Lake Street, Suite 100
Oak Park, Illinios 60301
"Bosc Directory"
Compiled and Edited by Irene Slovak
Bosc Publishers
Box 305
Cowgers, New York 10420
"Campus Access for Learning Disabled Students"
Barbara Scheiber, Jeanne Talpers
Closer Look, 1985
The Parents' Campaign for Handicapped Children and Youth
1201 16th Street, N.W.
Washington, D.C. 20036
"College and the Learning Disabled Student"
Charles T. Mangrum II, Stephen S. Strichart
Grune & Stratton, Inc., 1984
Orlando, Florida 32887
"The F.C.L.D. Guide for Parents of Children with Learning
Disabilities"

F.C.L.D., 1985
99 Park Avenue
New York, New York 10016

RESIDENTIAL PROGRAMS / CAREER TRAINING

Chapel Haven
  1040 Whalley Avenue
  New Haven, Connecticut 06516
  (203/397-1714)
  A maximum of 37 L.D. residents, age 18–30, live in two- to four-bedroom apartments in a contemporary brick building. Privately funded. Founded in 1972 by parents of developmentally disabled children attending Maplebrook School in Amenia, New York. The directors are Jeanne and Ronald Bercowitz.
Jewish Special Young Adults (JESPY) House
  65 Academy Street
  South Orange, New Jersey 07079
  (201/762-6909)
  A maximum of 21 L.D. Jewish adults, age 18–30, live in apartments, each containing three, four, or five people. Jewish identity is encouraged as a tool to help the resident develop self-confidence. Privately funded. Founded in 1978 by parents of L.D. children in Camp Ramah, New York. Carol and Steve Goodman are the directors.
Life Development Institute
  P.O. Box 15112
  Phoenix, Arizona 85060
  (602/955-2920, 602/956-8334)
  The Life Development Institute features a Post-secondary Prep Program, a Life Skills Training Program with a residential option, and a Model for Employment and Adult Living (MEAL). Clients live in an apartment setting while they learn. Robert Crawford is the director.
Para Educator Center for Young Adults

New York University
One Washington Place
New York, NY 10003
A two-year, post-high school program which trains L.D. young adults for work with young children, senior citizens, and in other helping professions. Judith Kranes is the director.

Success Through Independent Living Experience
(STILE)
MACLD Apartment Residence
1501 Park Avenue
Asbury Park, New Jersey 07712
(201/774-4737)
Two L.D. residents live in each of the nine garden apartments. They are 18–26 years old. Privately funded. Founded in 1979 by Monmouth County ACLD. William Buffton is the director.

Terry's Residence for Young Adults (TYRA) Hostel
14 Elk Street
Hempstead, New York 11550
(516/481-3833)
Thirty-one residents live on the second floor of a three-story apartment house. Nondisabled tenants live on the other two floors. It is funded by a combination of state and private funds. The clients pay half of their tuition from their social security income or competitive employment. The State of New York matches that amount. Parents are not required to pay tuition. Founded by Nassau County Chapter of ACLD. Ann Shields is the director.

Woodrow Wilson Rehabilitation Center
Box 125
Fishersville, Virginia 22939
Excellent training programs in social skills and job training.

"Learning Disabled Adults Face the World of Work"
Dale Brown
A.L.D.A.
P.O. Box 9722

Friendship Station
Washington, D.C. 20016
"National Directory: Training and Employment Programs for
  Americans with Disabilities"
United States Department of Education
400 Maryland Ave., S.W.
Washington, D.C. 20200

ADULT GROUPS

The growth of groups for adults with learning disabilities has
been rapid. There are now national networks and organizations,
some of which are affiliated with the Association for Children with
Learning Disabilities (ACLD) and some of which are not. Their
purposes include self-help seminars, group activities, dissemina-
tion of information, and social opportunities. Most are listed in one
or more of the national networks bulletins. Here are some.

Adelphi Learning Disabled Adult Organization
  Adelphi Social Service Center
  Adelphi University
  Garden City, New York 11530
  Nonnie Star, Program Coordinator of the Learning Disabled
A National Network of Learning Disabled Adults
  P.O. Box Z
  East Texas State University
  Commerce, Texas 75428
  John Moss
Association of Learning Disabled Adults (ALDA)
  P.O. Box 9722
  Friendship Station
  Washington, D.C. 20016
  Dale Brown
Institute for LD
  313 Caruth-O'Leary Hall

University of Kansas
Lawrence, Kansas 66103
Don Deshler

LAUNCH, Inc., The Coalition of LD Adults
Department of Special Education
East Texas State University
Commerce, Texas 75428
John R. Moss

Marin Puzzle People, Inc.
1368 Lincoln Avenue
San Rafael, California 94901
JoAnn Haseltine

Pennsylvania ACLD Youth and Adult Section
1108 Mayberry Lane
State College, Pennsylvania 16801
Melissa R. Holl

Phoenix, Arizona Sunshiners
2701 E. Camelback Road
Phoenix, Arizona 85061
Dorothy Crawford

Time Out To Enjoy, Inc.
113 Garfield Street
Oak Park, Illinois 60304
Jane Johnston

YACLD
210 Wick Avenue
Youngstown, Ohio 44503

RECORDED BOOKS AND MAGAZINES

"Talking Books"
Library of Congress, National Library Service for the Blind
and Physically Handicapped
1291 Taylor Street, N.W.

Washington, D.C. 20542
(202/822-5500)
Medical certification is necessary, but because of WHO (World
Health Organization) classification, this is now a simple proce-
dure. Forms are available from local libraries. Once people
have been accepted, they are issued a tape recorder and
books. These may simply be reregistered at a new library if a
person moves. Textbooks for school subjects may also be requested. If the book is currently available, it will be sent on
tape in about one month. If it is not available, send two copies
of the book. Books and completed tape will then be returned
in two to three months. No cost.
Recordings for the Blind, Inc.
215 East 58th Street
New York, New York 10002
(212/751-0860)
Disability must be certified by counselor or physician. Many
resources available. No cost.

FUNDING SOURCES AND EMPLOYMENT/JOB TRAINING

"Becoming Employable"
  Tri-SELPAS Job Project
  Acalanes Union High School District
  1212 Pleasant Hill Rd.
  Lafayette, California 94549
"Directory of Federal Aid for the Handicapped ($35.50). A Guide
  to Federal Assistance Programs Serving the Handicapped"
  Ready Reference Press, 1982
  P.O. Box 5097
  Santa Monica, California 90405
"Need a Lift? To Educational Opportunities, Careers, Loans,
  Scholarships, Employment." An American Legion Service for
  Young People (31st ed.), 1982

American Legion National Emblem Sales Division
P.O. Box 1055
Indianapolis, Indiana 46206
"Transition and Employment Skills Training to Special and
Vocational Education Teachers"
Tri-SELPAS Job Project
Acalanes Union High School District
1212 Pleasant Hill Rd.
Lafayette, California 94549
"What Do You Do After High School?" ($24.95)
Skyer Consultation Center
P.O. Box 121
Rockaway Park, New York 11694
Nationwide guide to residential, vocational, social, and collegiate programs serving the adolescent, young adult, and adult with L.D.

GENERAL INTEREST

"Educational Opportunities for Handicapped Students"
1981 (idea handbook for colleges and universities)
Academy for Educational Development
S. Tickton, W. Kinder, and A. Foley
1414 22nd Street, N.W.
Washington, D.C. 20037
"Employment Considerations for L.D. Adults" and "Self-help
Groups for L.D. People and the Rehabilitation Process"
D. Brown, *Journal of Rehabilitation*, Vol. 50, No. 4, April,
May, June, 1984
"How to Spell It"
Harriet Wittels and Joan Greisman
Grosset and Dunlap, New York
"Independent Living and L.D. Adults,"
American Rehabilitation, Vol. 7, No. 6, July, August, 1982.
Reprinted as a booklet by the President's Committee on

Employment of the Handicapped, 1984. Reprinted *Their World: A Publication of the Foundation for Children With Learning Disabilities*, 1984.

Independent Living Ideas, Marketing Your Disability . . . and Yourself, brochure published by President's Committee on Employment of the Handicapped, 1983. Reprinted *Dialogue*, Vol. 22, No. 3, Fall, 1983.

"Independent Living Skills Can Be Taught," *National*, Vol. 19, No. 1, Summer, 1982.

"Independent Living for L.D. Adults, An Overview" Chapter of *Early Adolescence to Early Adulthood, Vol. 5, The Best of ALCD*, William M. Cruikshank (with Carol Goodman, Stephen Goodman, and William Buffton) Syracuse University Press, 1984

"I'd Like It If I Could Learn It!" (Finger Multiplication/Math Skills) Barbara Cordoni *Academic Therapy Publications* 20 Commercial Blvd. Novato, CA 94947-6191

"Job Finding Skills and L.D. Adults," *Vocational Education, New and Related Services Insider*, Vol. 52, No. 2, March, 1982. (with Marjorie Rust and Robert Ruffner)

"Learning Despite L.D.," chapter in *Helping the Learning Disabled Student*, by Marlin R. Schmidt, Hazel Z. Sprandel, Jossey–Bass Publishers, 1982.

"Learning Disabilities," "Post-Secondary Options for Learning Disabled Students," and "Vocational Education for Learning Disabled Students," *Fact Sheets* by Educational Resources Information Center (ERIC), 1980.

"Learning Disability: Not Just a Problem Children Outgrow" President's Committee on Employment of the Handicapped Superintendent of Documents U.S. Government Printing Office Washington, D.C. 20402

"Learning to Dance," *Churchill Forum*, March 1983. Reprinted

Their World, A Publication of the Foundation for Children with Learning Disabilities, 1984.

"Profile of Learning Disabled Persons in the Rehabilitation Program," *American Rehabilitation*, Lawrenceville, Massachussetts, July–August–September, 1986.

"Programs for the Handicapped"
Clearinghouse on the Handicapped
Room 3130 Switzer Building
Washington, D.C. 20202

"Recollections," *Academic Therapy*, Vol. 15, No. 3, January, 1980.

Rehabilitating the L.D. Adult, booklet published by President's Committee on Employment of the Handicapped, August, 1982.

"Serving the L.D. Student in a Vocational Educational Classroom"
ERIC Clearinghouse on Handicapped and Gifted Children
1920 Association Drive
Reston, Virginia 22091

"Steps to Independence for People with L.D."
D. Brown
Health/Closer Look Resource Center
P.O. Box 1492
Washington, D.C. 20013

"The Learning Disabled Adult: An Administrative Challenge," *American Rehabilitation*, Vol. 8, No. 2, November, December, 1982.

"The Learning Disabled Young Adult," chapter in *Mainstreaming: A Concept in Faculty Preparation*, by Barbara K. Given, published by Office of Special Education Programs, US Department of Education, August, 1983.

"Typing Keys Program for the Remediation of Reading and Spelling Difficulties"
Maetta Davis
Academic Therapy Publications

20 Commercial Blvd.
Novato, CA 94947–6191

INFORMATION SOURCES

Association for Children and Adults with Learning Disabilities
(ACLD)
4156 Library Road
Pittsburgh, Pennsylvania 15234
(412/341-1515)
ACLD has publications available, lists of references, informa-
tion on local, state, and national chapters, and much more.
Directory of Facilities and Services for the Learning Disabled
Academic Therapy Publications
20 Commercial Boulevard
Novato, California 94947
(415/883-3314)
The Foundation for Children with Learning Disabilities
99 Park Avenue
New York, New York 10016
(212/687-7211)
The Orton Dyslexia Society
724 York Road
Baltimore, Maryland 21204
(301/296-0232)
The Orton Dyslexia Society has information on state, local,
and national affiliates; a list of publications; its own journal,
and much more.

.Barbara Cordoni's career has been distinguished by excellence as teacher, lecturer, contributor to numerous professional journals, and consultant on learning disabilities to colleges and universities throughout the country. She is the recipient of many honors and awards from teaching and professional associations, including several Distinguished Teacher of the Year awards and the Wallace Phillips Memorial Award for Outstanding Service in the Field of Learning Disabilities. A Professor in the Department of Special Education, Southern Illinois University, she is Coordinator of the Clinical Center Achieve Program for persons with learning disabilities. She established the program in 1978 and it became a permanent part of the university structure in 1983, making it the first L.D. program to be incorporated into a university.